Hold Successful Meetings

Caterina Kostoula is an executive coach and founder of The Leaderpath, a leadership coaching company. She has worked as a Global Business Leader at Google where she was also a 5-star rated internal coach. She has coached leaders and teams from Google, Amazon, Vodafone and Workable, as well as a number of startups. She is a member of the Forbes Coaches Council and coaches for INSEAD and Hult Ashridge Business School. Her work has been featured in *Forbes*, *Fast Company* and *Thrive Global*.

Caterina holds an MBA from INSEAD and an MSc in executive coaching from Hult Ashridge Business School. She has lived in more than seven countries across America, Europe and Asia and is currently based in London.

Caterina Kostoula

Hold Successful Meetings

BUSINESS

PENGUIN BUSINESS EXPERTS

UK | USA | Canada | Ireland | Australia
India | New Zealand | South Africa

Penguin Business Experts is part of the Penguin Random
House group of companies whose addresses can
be found at global.penguinrandomhouse.com.

Penguin
Random House
UK

First published 2021
001

Copyright © Caterina Kostoula, 2021

The moral right of the author has been asserted

Text design by Richard Marston
Set in 11.75/14.75pt Minion Pro
Typeset by Jouve (UK), Milton Keynes
Printed and bound in Italy by Grafica Veneta S.p.A.

The authorized representative in the EEA is
Penguin Random House Ireland, Morrison Chambers,
32 Nassau Street, Dublin D02 YH68

A CIP catalogue record for this book is available
from the British Library

ISBN: 978–0–241–48195–0

Follow us on LinkedIn: https://www.linkedin.com/
company/penguin-connect/

www.greenpenguin.co.uk

MIX
Paper from
responsible sources
FSC
www.fsc.org   FSC® C018179

Penguin Random House is committed to a
sustainable future for our business, our readers
and our planet. This book is made from Forest
Stewardship Council® certified paper.

I dedicate this book to my mother, Olga Rakka, for her unconditional love and support.

Author's Note

This book contains many strategies and techniques derived from real-life situations that I have encountered during my coaching sessions. Details have been changed, where appropriate, to protect the privacy of individuals and organizations.

Contents

List of Figures

List of Tables

Introduction

It was a Monday in October 2017. As I looked at my calendar, I felt a tightening in my chest. My day was packed with internal meetings. I was a business leader in the global sales team at Google, based in London, and most of my internal meetings were virtual. Like many of us working in big companies, I suffered from meeting fatigue.

Before every meeting, I braced myself. I felt a desperate need to escape. I would prefer a hundred times to be focusing on my clients, doing my own work or even meeting all of my colleagues individually.

For a long time, I thought it was just me who found internal meetings insufferable. I was wrong – and definitely not alone. A staggering 46 per cent of employees would prefer to do almost anything else rather than attend a status meeting – 17 per cent of them would prefer to watch paint dry![1] The cost of poorly organized meetings in 2019 was estimated to nearly half a trillion dollars in the US and the UK alone, according to Doodle's meetings report.[2] This is nearly half a trillion dollars for these two countries alone – a tremendous loss for their economies and for the profitability of their businesses. Nonetheless, most companies invest little effort in helping people run better meetings.

Early in 2018, I left Google to build my coaching company,

The Leaderpath. My mission was to coach leaders in how to maximize their impact and fulfilment, supporting them to connect more meaningfully with themselves and others.

Soon enough, I realized that meetings were often at the centre of my work with my clients. As humans we have two deep psychological needs. The first one is the need to feel valued and accepted (love). The second is the need to feel that we can make a difference (power). When we come together with other people to work towards a common goal, we satisfy both of those needs. When we belong to a cohesive, value-creating team, we feel appreciated and powerful. We can achieve so much more through collaboration than we would on our own.

Nonetheless, most meetings fail to create the right conditions for collaboration. My clients often told me that their meetings were interrupting their 'real work'. Even though they spent their day in back-to-back calls, they complained of 'silos', 'disconnect' and 'loneliness'. Often, they felt ignored or stressed in their meetings. Meeting dysfunction led to team dysfunction and then to low business performance and misery.

To help my clients build stronger teams, I added team coaching to my services. Soon, I realized I loved running team coaching sessions. I saw my clients getting closer to their colleagues, having the difficult conversations they had been avoiding, and solving long-standing issues. The speed with which we would make progress was so much faster when we had all the players in the room. Participants mentioned that after these sessions they felt a renewed excitement about their work.

At some point, it dawned on me that team coaching sessions were also meetings. The difference was that, unlike most meetings, participants left those sessions with a sense of fulfilment – and this positive feeling trickled down to their own teams.

I got curious. What is the difference between mind-numbing

meetings and transformative meetings? Could we bring some of the characteristics of team coaching and facilitation to our everyday meetings, to make them more successful?

The complaints I most often hear about meetings fall into three categories.

- They are **ineffective** – these meetings do not achieve their desired outcome or they have no clear desired outcome to begin with.
- They are **miserable** – these meetings are difficult to get through because we feel bored, frustrated or stressed.
- They are **too frequent** – a lot of us have too many meetings.[3]

When your meetings are ineffective and miserable, you feel disconnected and powerless. Your team's and your own time and potential are being squandered.

This book will help you to solve these problems by looking after the Purpose, People and Process of your meetings. Meetings, by definition, are occasions when a group of people come together to discuss and achieve a particular Purpose. In Part One of this book we will look at why so many of the meetings we experience are chaotic, unproductive, boring or frustrating – and what to do about it. You will encounter the 4D Meeting Framework that will help you clarify and achieve your meeting's Purpose.

In Part Two, we will cover how to look after the People and the Process of our meetings. You can only achieve your meeting's Purpose when People feel they can bring their true and best selves to the meeting. We will also review Process strategies, including how you can reduce the number of wasteful meetings you have.

As a leader, your job is to guide a group towards a common goal. Bringing people together in real time to achieve a common goal – aka having a meeting – is arguably one of the most powerful tools in your leadership arsenal. This book will equip you to hold fewer, more successful meetings, which are fun and fulfilling for your participants and yourself. You will also learn how to improve your meetings, even if you are not the organizer yourself.

To accompany the book, I have created the quiz 'How Successful Are Your Meetings?' where you can find out what you do well in your meetings and where you may need to improve. You and your team can take the quiz at www.theleaderpath.com/meetings.

By the end of the book, you will have the practical tools to turn your meetings into a competitive advantage for your department and your business. Your meetings could be the place where work gets done, rather than interrupted. Your meetings could help build people's sense of belonging, rather than making them feel excluded, ignored, scared or bored.

Are you ready to turn your meetings into the best part of the week for everyone involved, and the place where you help bring the biggest difference in the world?

Let's make a start.

Caterina Kostoula

PART ONE

Purpose

In the first part of the book, we will look at how to successfully achieve your meeting's Purpose.

You will be introduced to the 4D Meeting Framework, which explains the four outcomes you can pursue in your meetings and how to make sure you achieve them.

| Figure 1: Purpose, People and Process Triangle

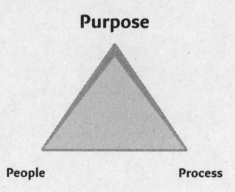

1   Meetings Matter

The benefits of good meetings

So why are we both here, spending our time trying to fix our meetings? Can't we simply remove meetings from our lives? I know I badly wanted to do that when I left corporate life. Well, the answer is: not if we want to make a difference. Humans have always changed the path of history by meeting with other people. While relatively powerless compared to other animals in a one-to-one setting, we have gained all our power through the ability to collaborate with each other. From deciding whether to go to war, to spearheading a ground-breaking new idea, societies leapfrog their evolution through meetings.

The quality of our meetings will define the impact of our career. Imagine if all the governments and political organizations held inclusive meetings where people could think, speak up, and contribute towards making the best decisions possible? Imagine if all businesses had meetings that truly leveraged the brainpower of their employees and partners in order to solve the most crucial problems? The world would be a better place.

We can eliminate a great number of useless meetings and replace them with more suitable alternatives. But meetings are still one of the best tools we have if we want to achieve one of the following:

- **Inspire action**. It is not easy to get people to change their behaviour. You have more chances of achieving it if you meet with them face-to-face. That is why politicians tour the country before elections. That is why companies invest in salespeople for high-priced items instead of simply relying on ads. If you want to influence people to do something, you are likely to be more successful if you meet with them.
- **Build a stronger connection**. We are social animals. And the way we have built a rapport for thousands of years is through meeting people face-to-face. The relationships with our clients, colleagues, suppliers or investors can make or break our company and career. Through meetings, rather than written communication alone, we can make our connection stronger.
- **Avoid misunderstandings and confusion**. A big part of our communication is done through our tone of voice and body language. How many times has your intention been misunderstood in an email and you've had to jump on a call to sort things out? When you need to communicate something, and you cannot afford confusion or misunderstanding, a meeting is likely to be your best bet.
- **Get inspired**. Author Charlie 'Tremendous' Jones said: 'You will be the same person in five years as you are today except for the people you meet and the books you read.'[1] We need external stimuli to spark our creativity and evolve our thinking. Creative meetings are one of the best ways to boost innovation and change in organizations.
- **Build a vibrant healthy culture**. How you do anything is how you do everything. How you run your meetings

is how you run your company. If you want a healthy culture that is inclusive, friendly, honest and creative, you will need to hold meetings that are too.

The concept of the 'lonely genius' is a myth. The companies who succeed are the ones who can harness the power of teamwork – the ones who fuel the diversity of thought and the creativity of groups – and make better decisions. Great companies understand this.

The cost of bad meetings

Great companies also understand that meetings are expensive – so they'd better create value. Bain Consultancy worked with a large manufacturing company when they discovered that a regularly scheduled ninety-minute meeting of mid-level managers cost more than $15 million annually.[2] When partner Michael Mankins asked them, 'Who is responsible for approving this meeting?' the managers were at a loss. 'No one,' they replied. 'Tom's assistant just schedules it, and the team attends.' In effect, a junior VP's administrative assistant was permitted to invest $15 million without supervisor approval![3]

Time is a zero-sum commodity, and you cannot get it back. While they are in meetings, salespeople do not pitch to clients. Software engineers do not write code. Doctors don't see patients. We need to make sure our meetings are at least worth the cost of our attendees' time.

It is not only the time people spend in meetings that has an opportunity cost. Paul Graham, co-founder of Y Combinator, argued that makers operate in half-day intervals. He called this a maker's schedule, which is different from a manager's schedule.[4] If you are a programmer or a writer and you have only an hour until your next meeting, you probably won't start working on your code or manuscript. This time is barely enough; it takes an hour to really get started. So, let's say you are a coder and you have a meeting scheduled at 10.30 a.m. There's not enough time to start working on a difficult coding problem before your meeting, and you probably won't get started after the meeting as there is not enough time before lunch. When you are a maker, and you have a half-hour meeting in your morning, you do not just lose the productivity of this half-hour. You are likely to lose half a day's productivity.

It is even worse when the meetings are bad. Psychologists have found that the effects of a bad meeting can linger for hours – a phenomenon called 'meeting recovery syndrome'. According to Joseph A. Allen, from the University of Utah, when an employee sits through an ineffective meeting, their brainpower is essentially being drained away.[5] After a lousy meeting, it is common for people to browse the internet to recover, go for a coffee, or go and interrupt a colleague to tell them about the meeting.

The cost of bad meetings is more than just financial. How your employees feel about their meetings correlates with how satisfied they are with their job. Studies show that bad meetings can make everyone feel less engaged and less happy with their jobs, even if they like their work, boss and colleagues. Given the negative impact ineffective meetings have on employees' job satisfaction, bad meetings may lead to higher attrition in your team. In addition, if you hold bad meetings, your reputation and potentially your career prospects will suffer. Professor Steven Rogelberg, who has researched meetings extensively, argues: 'There is perhaps no other work activity that is just so common, and yet so complained about.'[6] This means that the attendees of your meetings will not keep it to themselves if they are unhappy; they will complain about it.

The more meetings we have during our day, the more tired we feel by the end of it.[7] During meetings we feel a social pressure to perform and to project a certain image of ourselves. Meetings are our 'stage' as business people, and they can be tiring. Meetings require us to focus, actively listen, absorb information and think how to respond. If we have meetings with direct reports and clients, we strive to empathize with them, which can lead to compassion fatigue (already well documented among carers, such as therapists or nurses).

Back-to-back meetings are even more exhausting. Professor Gloria Mark, from the University of California, found that it takes us around twenty-three minutes to get back to a task after an interruption; we need this much time to successfully switch context and focus. Having back-to-back meetings makes us less effective and more tired. Our mind feels the need to digest what happened in the last meeting while we push our attention forward to the new meeting. The fatigue is worse when meetings are virtual, as we make an extra effort to overcome the lack of body language cues, and to deal with technical issues that arise. When we have too many ineffective meetings, we accomplish less during the day, and we may feel an obligation to work in the evening. This lack of recharging time can eventually lead to burnout.

Changing bad meetings into good

Changing your meetings is the first domino that will have a knock-on effect throughout your business and your life. By increasing the quality of your meetings, you will increase the quality of your work, business and life.

We both want the meetings we run and the meetings we participate in to be better. We both believe that meetings should move everyone ahead rather than waste their time. We want people to look forward to our meetings and get value out of them.

Most managers do not know that their meetings are bad. Bosses consistently rate their meetings better than other people's.[8] The more someone talks in a meeting, the more they tend to like it,[9] and the leader is usually the one who speaks the most. I acknowledge you for understanding the importance of meetings, and for wanting to improve them. Doing so will set you apart from the majority of leaders out there.

It's now time to introduce the 4D Meeting Framework.

2 The 4D Meeting Framework

The origins of the Framework

I was observing the meeting of a marketing leadership team. They wanted to launch some new webinars for their clients. In the meeting, the group got stuck: they could not agree on how to invite the clients to the webinars, as they had multiple booking systems. The leader tried to help the group make a quick decision as she had more important things to tackle on the agenda. She suggested a vote between two options. Before the participants started voting, one of them suggested a new solution. Then another participant argued that she did not see a problem at all, and she could not understand why they were having that discussion. The fourth participant was trying to iron out the details of implementing one of the solutions.

After some time, the leader chose one of the options and asked the group for an agreement to move forward. Once again, the creative participant threw a new idea on to the table. The group started discussing again, and by the end of the meeting no decision had been made. The team would have to tackle this in a follow-up meeting. What's more, there was no time to discuss more critical items on the agenda.

What went wrong in that meeting? Why was a team of brilliant leaders unable to solve a seemingly simple issue?

The key problem was that the participants were trying to achieve different goals. The leader of the team was trying to make a decision. One participant was attempting to ideate solutions, a third participant did not see a problem at all, and the fourth participant was concerned about the implementation. This happens all too often in meetings.

As individuals, we do not solve problems in a linear way. We jump from generating ideas to deciding that they are no good, then maybe going back to defining the problem better, coming up with new ideas, and so on. Imagine that you are in the UK and you think about where to go on holiday. The Caribbean comes to your mind. As you think about planning your trip, you realize that maybe the Caribbean is too far, so you go back to redefining the problem. Where can you go on holiday with a shorter than five-hour flight. You go back to ideation mode and create a list of options, such as Spain and Italy. As you try to decide, a new idea, Greece, springs to mind and you add it in. You move back and forth between Defining the problem, Developing solutions, and Deciding. It is an intuitive process that works well at an individual level, but creates chaos at a group level.

Al Pittampalli, founder of the Modern Meeting Company, argues that a lot of the chaos in meetings happens because participants start the discussion at different problem-solving stages. Then, they keep moving back and forth between the stages, without their fellow participants knowing. 'The result is a disorganized meeting that traverses many stages, yet conquers none,' Pittampalli says.[1]

Solving a problem in meetings often feels like such a mountainous task. It is not because of malice or incompetence; it is simply because we try to solve problems intuitively, instead of having a structure that allows the participants to work towards the same outcome at the same time.

I developed the 4D Meeting Framework to overcome that challenge, and it will transform your meetings. If you adopt it, you will go from feeling that you are herding cats, to leading a productive group that gets work done. You will help your attendees feel like they are part of a team that makes a difference.

The four pillars of the Framework

The 4D Meeting Framework aligns the participants on what they are aiming to achieve in every stage of a meeting. Successful meetings achieve one or more of four key outcomes:

- **Define** (a problem or a goal)
- **Develop** (ideas)
- **Decide**, or
- **Do**.

That's all. Simple and easy to remember. You can have a meeting to achieve only one of the 4Ds. Or, if you want to achieve more than one in your meeting, you should do it in clearly defined stages.

Let's take a closer look at the 4Ds.

- **Define** the problem or goal. In a Define meeting (or meeting stage), you get to the crux of the issue or topic under discussion. What is going on now? What should we try to achieve? What is the key obstacle? Defining the problem is a crucial outcome. You don't want to waste time trying to solve the wrong problem. In the Define chapter, you will learn how to create a

| Figure 2: The 4D Meeting Framework

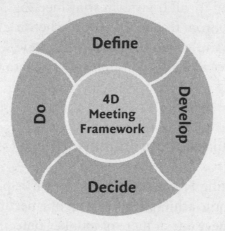

shared view of reality, a common vision for the future, and clarity about the problem you need to solve.

- **Develop** ideas. In a Develop meeting (or meeting stage), the group comes up with various ideas to solve the problem. Most groups either fail to spend time here generating enough options to solve their problem, or they resort to traditional brainstorming that does not work. In the Develop chapter, we will review what works instead. The outcome of a Develop meeting or meeting stage is a list of ideas.
- **Decide** the way forward. In a Decide meeting (or meeting stage), you select which of the ideas you are going to pursue. Many business decisions fail. In the Decide chapter, I will share the different ways you can make decisions in your meetings, and how you can mitigate the bias that can lead to wrong decisions. You will also learn how to handle productive conflict that enhances the quality of your decision making without

turning your meeting nasty. The outcome here is a decision.

- **Do!** A Do meeting (or meeting stage) is about action – during or after the meeting. Do meetings can include working sessions, inspiring talks and action-planning workshops. While in the previous Ds you look to unearth the differences in opinion and perspective, you now want to align people so you can move forward in a joint course of action. We will see how in the Do chapter.

When Doodle researched over 16,000 meetings, they found that the number one way to improve meetings was to have clear objectives.[2] The 4Ds are outcomes to pursue in your meetings and also steps in a process. To solve any problem, you must inevitably Define it, Develop ideas, Decide the way forward, and Do what you decided. I suggest you let your participants know in advance which of the Ds you will be pursuing in the meeting. This will help them prepare and also be clear and focused on the outcome(s) you want the meeting to achieve.

Avoid confusion during the meeting by letting the group know when you are transitioning from one D to another. In this way, everyone will understand what you are trying to achieve at any given point in the meeting.

The benefits of the 4D Meeting Framework

By following the 4D Meeting Framework, you will improve the quality of your discussions and also reduce the time you waste in your meetings. With the 4D Meeting Framework, you will enjoy your meetings more and you will stop wasting time in unnecessary ones. The perception around meetings in your organization will change.

You will avoid meetings that could have been an email

Most communication between people does not need to be synchronous. Sharing the status of a project rarely needs to happen in real time. For every one of the 4Ds, synchronous communication can bring to the surface valuable insights, ideas and opinions, and helps you to achieve buy-in from people.

You will benefit from everyone's brainpower in your meeting

If the issue is not relevant to all attendees, there will be a waste of time and a sense of disengagement. When you are having a 4D meeting and you have the right list of attendees, everyone can and should participate.

You will reduce the need to schedule additional meetings

A poorly facilitated meeting will require more meetings to achieve a desired outcome. By following the 4Ds Framework, you are more likely to avoid unnecessary follow-ups. The structure and the clarity about the desired outcome of the meeting will help your participants stay focused and productive.

Preparing to put the Framework into practice

I suggest you go through your calendar and label your meetings with the D-outcomes they are meant to pursue. You can also challenge the organizers of any scheduled meetings to clarify the purpose of their meeting – and, if there is no clear purpose, whether the meeting is needed at all. A meeting can have more than one D as a desired outcome. But if a meeting does not have any of the 4Ds, look into whether you need that meeting at all. In Chapter 9, I will show how you can use information sharing, socializing, and more, to replace meetings that do not have any D-outcomes.

Now that you have cleared your calendar of unnecessary meetings, and have clarified the desired outcome for every one of the meetings you've kept, we are ready to move on to the first of the Ds. Let's learn how you can successfully achieve a Define outcome in your meeting.

3   Define the Problem or the Goal

I was coaching an engineering leadership team that struggled with its workload not being equally distributed among its teams. The leaders came to the meeting thinking that they would need to decide on a new organizational structure. As we delved more into the problem, we realized that their product priorities constantly changed, making their organizational structures quickly antiquated. They could temporarily solve their current challenge by redistributing their engineers, but they were bound to face the same problem in a few months' time. The initial problem statement was: 'What should our new structure look like?' After we spent time on Defining the problem, we ended up with the following problem statement: 'How might we better align our resources to the evolving product priorities?'

If you define a problem correctly, the solution is a lot easier to find. In the engineering team's case, the problem definition pointed out that a more flexible structure would better suit that organization. They could assign engineers to the current product priorities, without committing them for the long term.

When you start a meeting, you have a topic on the agenda. Maybe a question. Defining the goal or the problem is not the same as the agenda topic or the desired outcome for the meeting. For example, you may have convened a meeting because your sales conversion rates are down. This is the topic. During the Define stage of your meeting you may realize that the problem is that a certain salesperson is not performing well. You frame the problem as: 'How might we help John convert more sales calls?' The desired outcome of the meeting can be a list of ideas on how to help John.

The idea of defining a problem by starting with the three words 'How might we' originated at Procter & Gamble in the 1970s and was popularized by the company IDEO. By starting your problem definition with 'How might we', you already frame it as an opportunity – and one that is almost irresistible to try to solve. The more specific you are, the better. For example, you can say: 'How might we reduce our IT costs by 10 per cent?' or 'How might we acquire new clients in the Education sector?'

I suggest three steps in defining your problem:

- create a shared view of reality
- agree on what success looks like, and
- form a problem statement.

You do not need to do all these steps in every Define meeting, or do them in that order. I have used that sequence many times, because the problem emerges more clearly when we become aware of the gap between reality and our goal. Let's see how you go through these steps in your meeting.

Create a shared view of reality

Before you venture into solving a problem or agreeing on a desirable future, it is worth making sure everyone is on the same page about what is happening right now.

You may have circulated information – facts, data, analysis – before the meeting or gone through it at the start. It is important to allow participants time to digest the information so that everyone is abreast of the facts. Discussion in the meeting can then focus on any insights that arise.

During the meeting, you may want to invite participants to share any information they are privy to. It is well documented that groups spend most of their time talking about information that is shared, rather than revealing information that is known to only one individual. This is known as the 'hidden profiles' bias, and it negatively affects the success of the meeting.[1]

You also need to create awareness about how people feel about a certain topic, especially if it is a sensitive one. There are three techniques you can use to create a shared view of reality.

Invite perspectives

You can use a series of questions to reveal the participants' knowledge and opinions. Here are some examples.

- What do you want to say about the topic?
- What do you want to hear about the topic?
- What do you want to take out of the discussion?
- What is working well right now?
- What is not working well?
- What have we tried so far, and what have we learned?

After hearing the views of those in the meeting, you may want to bring in the voices of other stakeholders who are impacted by the topic of your meeting but are not present. In order to frame the problem and the goal, you often need to understand the stakeholders' point of view and what their challenges are.

A common technique we use at team coaching sessions is to include one or two empty chairs representing the group's key stakeholders, such as customers, investors, etc. At certain points in the meeting, you can ask the participants to sit in that chair and share the stakeholder's view about what is being discussed. At a virtual meeting, you can ask the participants to change their names on the video call to 'investor', 'employee', 'customer', and so on, and share the key stakeholders' perspectives.

In the meeting, there is often tension because people speak on behalf of those who are not in the room, but they do not make it explicit. You have HR people representing the interests of the employees, finance people representing investors, and so on. By explicitly stating that we represent other voices in the meeting, the other participants do not take what we say personally. We can be more honest and upfront when we represent someone else.

In a team coaching session with a product leadership team, we worked on improving performance. I asked the team what other voices we needed to hear. The vice-president of design asked to speak on behalf of her designers. She changed her name on the video call to 'designer'. She then went on to share an emotional statement: 'As a designer, I feel frustrated. You tenured designers have made a lot of mistakes, and I want to fix them, but I have no way of getting design fixes into the product roadmap. Then, I see in the net-promoter-score surveys that our software users do not like our user interface, and I get disheartened.' If she had shared this argument as her opinion, her colleagues on the product leadership team could have perceived it as exaggerated and too emotional. But, by sharing it as a designer, they were a lot more open to it, and they understood the frustration of her team better.

Use constellations

Constellations can be a quick and fun way to gather a lot of information about where the group stands on an issue. With a constellation, you ask the group to physically vote with their feet, to choose a space in the room that reveals what they think about the topic. If the meeting is remote, you can use a virtual whiteboard where people can position a Post-it note or a dot in a two-dimensional space.

The leader of a consumer goods company I was working with was worried that his team was not innovative enough. I wanted to quickly get a grasp on whether the group agreed with this assessment. In the team coaching session, I wrote the word 'innovation' on a piece of A4 paper and put it on the floor. I asked the group to stand up. Then I read out a series of statements and, depending on their level of agreement with each statement, they would place themselves closer to the word 'innovation' or further away.

The first statement was: 'We are an innovative team.' It was quickly obvious that people did not all have the same perception. Some thought that they were an innovative team and stood close to the word 'innovation', while others did not. I asked some volunteers from the extreme positions to elaborate on their point of view, providing more context to explain why they were standing where they were.

The second statement was: 'I contribute to the team's innovation.' After people had positioned themselves according to their perception, we sat down and explored what was causing the disparity of views around the team. It turned out that each member had a different view on what innovation was. With that insight, we were able to build bridges between the different perspectives, providing a solid foundation to move on to the next stages of the meeting: develop ideas, decide and plan on how to be more innovative.

Can you think of an opportunity when you might use constellations in your meetings?

Act as a mirror to the group

Another way to increase the group's awareness is to act like a mirror. Reflect back what you see and hear in the meeting. Summarize. Share your observations. You will be surprised how often a group is unaware of tension or intense emotions building up. By calling attention to it, you create awareness that people care deeply about the topic. And by naming it, you help ease any tension.

In June 2019, I ran a workshop at the INSEAD Alumni Forum in Geneva on how to be an inclusive leader. Initially, I thought that this should be a Do meeting: I needed to inspire my audience to behave as more inclusive leaders. After some thought, I realized that the challenge with bias in organizations is that it is unconscious. Everyone thinks they are already an inclusive leader; that is why very little changes. My goal became to help the participants see that they were part of the problem – we all are. We all have unconscious biases. I decided to do an exercise that would hold a mirror to the group.

I asked the audience to raise their hands if they believed that LGBTQ+ employees should have equal rights in the workplace. All one hundred attendees raised their hands. Then I asked them to open their phones and post on their LinkedIn feeds the following statement in their own words: 'Happy Pride! Let's all do our part to ensure every LGBTQ+ employee feels included in the workplace.' Around five people out of the hundred published the post. I explained that, as they had just experienced, it is not always easy to be public about our values and to share what we believe is right. Many of us are too afraid of being judged. If it was so hard for us to show public support as allies to the LGBTQ+ community, it is a lot harder for under-represented groups to ask for support. This exercise helped create awareness that there was bias, and also discomfort. People were more open to solving the problem in the rest of the workshop now that there was no denying that the issue existed.

Agree on what success looks like

Once you have helped the participants of your meeting create a shared view of reality, you are ready to look into the desired future.

Steve Jobs, former Apple CEO, said: 'It's okay to spend a lot of time arguing about which route to take to San Francisco when everyone wants to end up there, but a lot of time gets wasted in such arguments if one person wants to go to San Francisco and another secretly wants to go to San Diego.'² This happens all too often in meetings.

One of my consultant clients does the same exercise in every boardroom he enters: he asks people to write on a Post-it note what success looks like for the team. He says he has never found a team where people all wrote the same thing. Whether it is the vision for the company, the team, or the project at hand, a big part of the Define stage is to align the participants' definition of success. You need to have a clear destination.

You can do this top-down or bottom-up. In the top-down approach, the leader shares her vision. Then the team can ask questions, comment, express concerns, or build on it. By allowing this process to happen, you can achieve more buy-in from the group. In the bottom-up approach, you will need to help participants define their individual vision first and then create a shared vision. You can use questions or artefacts to help participants come up with their individual vision.

Focus on the what and not the how (for now)

When you build a vision of success, you are better off focusing on the 'what' rather than the 'how'. Set aside the strategy for a moment. Paint a picture of a desirable future, and you will be surprised by how readily you think of ideas you didn't know were possible before.

Peter Hawkins, leadership professor at Henley Business School,[3] told me that the purpose of the team should be arrived at by thinking 'future-back and outside-in'. What do the stakeholders need from the group? What does the future require?

Here are some additional key questions you can ask the participants, to help them articulate their vision.

- What does success look like for this project?
- Imagine that everything goes as well as you could possibly expect. How would this process/business/etc. look a year from now?
- If this issue was resolved, how would we know?

You can ask people to write down their vision and then share it with the group.

Make your vision tangible

When it comes to defining a vision, working with images, metaphors and symbols can be illuminating. Try some of the following suggestions:

- Ask people to draw their vision and share their drawings with the group.
- Use a deck of abstract photos (you can buy one online). Ask people to pick the picture that best represents their vision for the company, team or project.
- Use Lego bricks. This is one of my favourite methods, as people tend to be less self-conscious with Lego bricks than with drawing. I suggest you work in the beginning with a trained Lego Serious Play facilitator; they can train the participants quickly in how to use the bricks to represent anything.
- Make creative use of other materials. You can use Post-it notes, playdough, objects, etc.

Asking people to create or select something tangible – a drawing, a card, or a Lego model – has many benefits. You transfer more information than you would with just words. Everyone gets to participate and share, so you are inherently inclusive. Another benefit is that when you start debating the different visions, you can refer to the models rather than to the people who created them. This helps to make the discussion less tense or personal.

After you have helped people formulate and share their individual visions, you can start discussing the similarities and differences, and guiding people to a shared vision.

Team coach Georgina Woudstra argues that making your personal visions explicit can help diminish criticism and misunderstandings among the team members. She was coaching a team of three executives and asked them to draw their dream for the project at hand. The first drew the team receiving an award. The second drew the team coming down together from a ski slope, celebrating their success in a ski retreat. The third drew dollar signs and Excel spreadsheets. This exercise revealed each individual's motivations. It helped them avoid conflicts, with everyone pulling in a different direction. The team committed to helping each other achieve their goals. They could help the team win more money and awards. And when this was done, they would all go skiing!

Form a problem statement

Now that you have a clear vision of where you are and where you want to go, you can define the problem you need to solve in order to get there.

I observed a virtual meeting of an advertising agency team as they were trying to improve their pitching process. The team created a shared reality by answering questions such as: 'What is working in our pitches?', 'What is not working?', 'What does efficiency mean?', etc. The insights that emerged were that too many people participated in the pitch-preparation meetings, making them less efficient. Also, the executives were making late changes to the direction of the pitch, resulting in a lot of wasted work.

Instead of reviewing the issues identified, selecting the most important, and creating a problem statement, the team jumped into the brainstorming phase. They used the generic problem statement: 'How might we make our pitches great again?' After they had compiled a long list of ideas, they voted for the best idea, which was to use a 'police investigation board' – you know, the ones with photos, pins, and threads connecting the related topics – during their pitch preparation. The winning idea, while useful at maintaining the big picture of the project, did not solve any of the most pressing problems they had identified.

I see this phenomenon of not defining the problem in a precise manner in most of the meetings I observe. This often results in each participant trying to solve a different issue. Or, as we saw in the example above, the group comes up with a solution that does not address the real problem.

A full 85 per cent of C-suite executives agreed in a survey that their organizations were bad at problem diagnosis, and 87 per cent thought that this flaw carried significant costs.[4] The situation is exacerbated by the fallacy of: 'The sooner the project is started, the sooner it will be finished.'[5] It is tempting to skip to the solution-finding stage as quickly as possible.

Here are some ways that you can help the group define the problem they want to tackle.

Search for the root causes

It is worth exploring whether the issue at hand is a symptom of a different problem. The 'five whys' technique is popular here. You ask 'why?' five times, until you reach the root cause of the problem.

In the example of the agency that wanted to improve their pitching process, one of the problems was that the executives often appeared in pitches when the work had already started, resulting in changing direction too late. When the team discussed the issue further, they realized that the executives missed the initial meetings because each executive had to support many pitches happening at the same time. Going deeper, they saw that the company was taking on too many pitches. Now the problem could be defined as: 'How might we choose fewer pitches in which to participate?'

Find the exceptions to the problem

What are the situations where the problem does not exist? When are things working in the way they should? I was coaching a leader of a community of twenty people who were tasked with a digital transformation project. Out of those twenty people, five were part of the global central team while the other fifteen were in their local markets, reporting to their local managers.

The leader of this community thought that the local members were not engaged enough with the transformation project. This was a big problem for him as his performance was judged by how successful this community was. I asked him whether he saw any exceptions to his observation. Were some local community members more engaged than others? He realized that when the local managers had a strong relationship with their global counterparts, the engagement was a lot higher. With that insight, he could define the new challenge as: 'How might we encourage better one-to-one relationships between the local managers and their global counterparts?'

Now, rather than large gatherings for the whole community, the solution was more one-to-one meetings between global and local community members, to build more trust and connection.

Look at the problem from different angles

In every problem, try to look at it from a different angle – incentives, processes, people or skills – and see whether you can uncover more insights. You may want to separate your group into subgroups and give each a different lens to look at the problem. A good question to consider here is: 'What is stopping us from achieving our goal?'

For example, many companies are currently trying to increase the number of women in senior positions. The majority have looked at it as a skills problem and launched leadership development and mentorship programmes for women. Others have seen it as a people problem and begun unconscious-bias training for their managers.

I have suggested that companies should see this as a process problem.[6] How can they bias-proof their hiring and promotion processes? By reframing the problem, they can come up with a whole new set of solutions – including blind interviews, bias busters in calibration sessions, and more quantitative data to judge performance – rather than personal opinions about the candidates' 'style' or 'presence'.

Bring in an outside perspective

Researcher Thomas Wedell-Wedellsborg argues that bringing in an outside perspective is the single most effective reframing practice for problems.[7] He shares a story about a leadership team discussing a new training scheme for their employees, to help them innovate. The CEO thought they needed an outside perspective, so he brought his assistant Charlotte to participate in the discussion. She was sceptical. She said she had seen many training initiatives in her time in the company, and she did not think that the employees would welcome a new set of buzzwords.

The team realized that they had defined the problem in the wrong way: they had seen their workforce's lack of skills as the issue, but in reality it was a lack of engagement and motivation. Once they defined the problem correctly, they focused on improving engagement. They gave employees more autonomy, flexible working, and moved towards more participative decision making. Soon, the engagement grew, and people started being a lot more innovative.

So, who can you bring into your meeting to give you a fresh perspective? Think of those on the periphery of your team, and ask for their reactions. This will give you the insight to define your problem more accurately.

Check the commitment to solving the problem

Often, when we fail to solve a problem, it is not for lack of good ideas about what to do, but for lack of motivation to follow through. After you have defined the problem, you need to make sure that you have the group's commitment to solving it. You can do that by asking a series of questions, such as: 'How important is this problem from 1 to 10?' or 'How urgent is this problem?'

If you sense that the commitment to solving the problem is low, it is worth reflecting on the cost of inaction. How will the situation look in one year's time if the group does nothing? What are the risks? Who will be impacted? While it is easy to see the cost of investing effort and money into solving a problem, sometimes the cost of not solving it is not that obvious. For example, we might be reluctant to launch a new product that will cannibalize some of our existing sales. By asking what the cost of inaction is, we can quickly see that a competitor might launch the product first and undermine our sales anyway. With this added insight, the commitment of the group to launching this new product becomes stronger. If, after some exploration, the group still does not feel strongly motivated to solve the problem, you can park it for now and redirect your efforts into addressing a more important problem.

Summary

The Define stage in your meeting is crucially important. It is when you align all the participants, creating a shared sense of where you are, where you are going and what needs to be solved in order to get there. Table 1 summarizes the techniques we have discussed in this chapter.

The clarity created during the Define stage is essential before you move into solution mode. Now that you have a clearly defined problem, you can move on to developing ideas to solve it.

| Table 1: The Define Stage

Create a shared view of reality	Agree on what success looks like	Form a problem statement
Invite perspectives Use constellations Act as a mirror to the group	Focus on the what and not the how (for now) Make your vision tangible	Search for the root causes Find the exceptions to the problem Look at the problem from different angles Bring in an outside perspective Check the commitment to solving the problem

4 Develop Ideas

After you have defined the problem, it is time to start developing your solutions. If the problem is important, it is worth spending time generating many ideas and exploring potential avenues.

Researchers studied the decisions made by a top management team at a German tech company over a period of eighteen months. They evaluated the quality of those decisions a few years later – when they could judge their outcomes. They found that increasing the number of ideas the team deliberated over, from one to two, improved the quality of their decisions sixfold.[1] The management team had even more success when they came up with three or more alternatives.

Marc Zornes knew that he wanted to build a business to solve one of the biggest problems of the world: food waste. The obvious approach was to build something to help farms reduce their food waste, as he knew a lot about farms from his previous job at McKinsey. But he wanted to develop and evaluate many ideas before committing the next few years of his life to building something. He bounced ideas around with his co-founder, Kevin Duffy, and a selected group of advisers. They could eliminate waste in the distribution chain from farms to markets. They could work to eliminate food waste in homes. They could create products from food waste. None of these ideas seemed to work for them. And then the winning idea was born. They could work to eliminate food waste in restaurants and the hospitality sector. They created Winnow, an AI-driven waste monitor and bin for commercial kitchens. Seven years later, they have saved more than 35 million meals and 60,000 tonnes of CO_2.[2]

In this chapter, we will see how creativity works, so that you have more of it in your meetings. We will also review the best in group facilitation techniques for transforming meetings and making ideation fun. Why are creativity and innovation so elusive in our meetings? That's what we are going to find out next.

Create the conditions for creativity in your meetings

Meetings play a crucial role in boosting your company's creativity. A team that works well together will produce more innovation than a lonely genius. Three professors from Northwestern University analysed 19.9 million scientific papers and 2.2 million patents over fifty years. They found that people working in teams produce research that is cited more than twice as often as the work of individuals.[3]

In the 1960s, NASA asked Dr George Land and Beth Jarman to develop a test that could assess the creative potential of NASA's rocket scientists and engineers. They put themselves to work and developed the test; it performed well, and it was highly predictive. But Land and Jarman were left with questions. Where does creativity come from? Was it a result of nature or nurture? They decided to give the same test to 1,600 five-year-olds. The test measured their ability to come up with new and creative solutions to problems. Guess what percentage of five-year-olds qualified as a creative genius? A whopping 98 per cent!

The researchers were so shocked that they made the study longitudinal and tested the same kids five years later, when they were ten years old. Now, only 30 per cent fell within the genius category of creativity. Another five years later, only 12 per cent of the fifteen-year-olds were imaginative geniuses. And as for the more than a million adults tested above the age of thirty? A sad 2 per cent. Where does our creativity go as we grow up? Do we lose it for ever? Dr Land believes we can still find the imagination of our inner five-year-old.[4] Here are some techniques you can try.

Embrace divergent thinking

Our brain has two ways of thinking: divergent and convergent. In the divergent way of thinking, we come up with alternatives. In the convergent way of thinking, we edit the alternatives. Scientists have observed in MRI scans how different parts of the brain light up when we engage in divergent or convergent thinking. When we try to do both of those things simultaneously, they work against each other. Unfortunately, this is what the educational system has trained us to do. In the classroom, we were asked to come up with solutions to problems, but these solutions needed to be correct. So we learned to censor and criticize every idea that came up in our minds. By practising divergent and convergent thinking at the same time, we became less innovative.

The same happens in most meetings. Someone brings an idea, and what happens? Others jump in to criticize it: 'We have tried this before!', 'We have never done anything like this before!', 'That's a dumb idea!', 'That's a great idea!', 'That will never work!', and so on. All this criticism at the divergent stage stifles creativity and innovation.

If we do not unlearn this unproductive way of working, our businesses and our careers will suffer. We need to separate divergent and convergent thinking in our meetings. That's one of the reasons why the 4D Meeting Framework is so effective. It separates the Develop and the Decide stages.

We need to forget the word 'but'. We cannot write and edit at the same time. We should keep our criticism for the next stage, when we need to Decide. At this point, we accept all the ideas, welcome them, and try to build on them. It is better to say 'yes, and' rather than 'yes, but'. We need to make it safe for people to share half-baked, unclear ideas.

Build on each other's ideas
To be able to facilitate successful Develop meetings, we need to adopt a special, creativity mindset first. Many beliefs that serve us well in day-to-day business will not help us in a Develop meeting. Commitment to high standards, for example, is great when you serve a customer. If you bring this value to the ideation session, though, it will stand in the way of people sharing ideas, for fear of being silly. We need to shift from the 'manufacturing' mentality – where all products need to meet a certain standard – to the 'creative process' mentality. We should only care about the quality of the winning idea; the rest can happily be flops, and it does not matter.

In a Develop meeting, you get exposed to new and unexpected ideas that may spark new responses in you. Think of the Wright brothers who, according to their journals, had an amazingly close collaboration when they invented the aeroplane. Think of John Lennon and Paul McCartney, who collaborated so closely in the creative process that all their songs had both names, and they shared the profits equally. Think about the last time you were part of a creative, non-hierarchical group that thrived on building on each other's ideas and taking them a step further. It is highly likely that you felt safe speaking up and sharing ideas in the group.

Be comfortable with inefficiency and uncertainty

Creativity is, by default, inefficient. Many ideas or paths will not be used in the end. Also, bear in mind that the creative process will benefit from the time between scheduled meetings. We may need to take breaks, or have shorter meetings with a gap in between. We have all had great ideas while walking or in the shower. Ideas often come when we are more relaxed and not actively working on the problem. Pauses and breaks may appear to be a waste of time but, in reality, they are increasing the odds of a breakthrough.

We also need to embrace uncertainty. There will be people in the group who are uncomfortable with not knowing what the solution is. These people have a strong personality characteristic called 'need for closure'.[5] They will want to select an idea and get on with implementing it quickly. For strategic decisions, it is important to have time to generate, explore and build on the group's ideas. The group may get excited about one of the first ideas to come up, and want to move on. You can help generate more ideas by asking 'What else?' Having a structured ideation process can help participants with a high need for closure to wait until the ideas are fully developed, because they know that the process has a structure and time boundaries.

Steer clear of hierarchies

Being too hierarchical can stand in the way of Developing ideas. The creative partnership needs to be equal, so that everyone can bring and support any ideas rather than trying to please the boss. Creative teams perform better when they organize themselves rather than when someone organizes them from above. According to Intuit's co-founder Scott Cook, Google's founders 'tracked the progress of ideas that they had backed versus ideas that had been executed in the ranks without support from above, and discovered a higher success rate in the latter category'.[6]

As business leaders, we face unprecedented challenges. We need more innovation than ever. Robots are replacing workers who merely follow orders and produce repeatable results. We need teams to dream up solutions that have never been done before. Facilitating Develop meetings is becoming ever more crucial. For group ideation to work, we need to change our mindset, to be open to all the ideas the team brings. To really want them.

How to facilitate group ideation

Once we have worked on our mindset, and are clear on the benefits of divergent thinking, we are ready to facilitate our Develop ideas meeting.

When we think about an ideation meeting, one word comes to mind: brainstorming. Brainstorming was invented in the *Mad Men* era of advertising, and the whole idea was to separate divergent and convergent thinking. The rules of the brainstorming session were simple: have a group share uncensored ideas, and produce a high quantity of them; build on each other's ideas; ban criticism. Brainstorming became popular, and most of us have experienced it in the workplace. It seemed like a great solution.

But there is a problem. Brainstorming rarely works. In fact, it can be a waste of time if you do not do it properly. A review of over 800 teams indicated that individuals are more likely to generate a higher number of original ideas when they *don't* interact with others.[7] Individual brainstorming, where people write down several ideas on a piece of paper, often produces more and better ideas than group brainstorming.[8]

Here are the four key reasons why traditional brainstorming does not work.

- **Social loafing**. This is a phenomenon that happens when people work in a group rather than individually. They do not have to work as hard, as there is less accountability, and they can hide behind the group's efforts.
- **Social anxiety**. People may be reluctant to share ideas if they are afraid of being judged by the group. Similarly, when team members perceive that others have more expertise, their performance declines.[9]
- **Regression to the mean**. The performance of the more talented and creative individuals in the group may converge towards the average. This also happens in sport. When you play a sport with a player worse than you, your performance declines.
- **Production blocking**. When people share their ideas verbally, they have to wait for their turn to talk. In the meantime, they may forget their ideas. They listen to other people's ideas, rather than producing their own, so overall, they produce fewer ideas.

How can you harness the power of the group in producing ideas, but avoid the brainstorming pitfalls? I suggest three key creative facilitation techniques. Let's look at each one in turn.

Come up with ideas individually first and then use small groups

Ask participants to write their ideas down on their own first. Allow silence for that to happen. Then invite the participants to share their ideas with the group, and build on them further.

INSEAD professor Karan Girotra found that teams using this hybrid approach – writing first, sharing second – were nearly three times as productive as group brainstorming teams. They also produced a winning idea of a higher quality, as judged by a crowdsourced survey.[10] This strengthens the case that we should have more meetings where individuals work individually first, whether reading the information or coming up with ideas.

If your team is remote, you can do electronic brainstorming using a tool to input ideas. There are many pieces of software available, some of them free of charge. You can find a selection at my 'Meeting Tools List' at www.theleaderpath.com/meetings. Participants enter their ideas on the software anonymously. With anonymity, there is no social anxiety. There is also no production blocking, as participants can enter ideas at the same time. Participants can be in a different country, and they can input their ideas at different times. Some programs show you other people's ideas, to simulate the inspiration that comes from others. Studies show that electronic brainstorming generates a higher quantity and a better quality of ideas than traditional brainstorming.[11]

Play some music while people are coming up with ideas individually. Keep it instrumental, so that it is not distracting – and in a major key, so the mood stays positive. You can also do some guided ideation. The traditional approach (encouraging a quantity of ideas, without offering any guidance) has worse results than approaches that provide more structure.[12] Share your constraints if you have them – particularly budget or infrastructure constraints – so people can focus on feasible solutions instead of wasting hours producing ideas that cannot be implemented.

Prepare some questions to guide people's creativity. When I was coaching a team that was trying to improve its way of working, I guided the ideation with three questions.

- How would you solve this if you were Apple?
- How would you solve this if you were the army and you needed military precision?
- How would you solve this if you were the Cirque du Soleil?

By changing its perspectives, the team was able to come up with fresher ideas than they would have done otherwise. For example, one participant had the idea of hiring mercenaries (contractors), inspired by the army question.

After the individual ideation, you can share and discuss your ideas with the group. If you are working with a big group, you may want to divide and conquer. Authors Kevin and Shawn Coyne suggest that you need to break your group into subgroups of between three and five people during ideation sessions.[13] They argue that the social norm is to speak up when there are fewer than five people, while for larger groups, it's to remain silent.

What you can also do is give the groups a different question around the same problem. For example, if you are a leadership team that wants to increase profitability, you can split into two groups. One group can look for ideas to increase revenue, while the other group can come up with ideas to reduce costs. After some time working in groups, everyone can join the wider group and share their ideas.

It works best if you isolate the idea-repellent individuals in their own subgroup. Idea repellents are people whose presence may make it more difficult for people to express ideas. These can be bosses, experts, or people who talk a lot. By putting them together in the same group, you help everyone else be productive – and they are less likely to deter each other from talking.

Make ideas tangible

A combination of drawing and writing works well for generating creative solutions to problems.[14] Psychology professor Art Markman argues that there are several reasons why drawing is helpful.

> First, it's hard for people to describe spatial relationships, so any solution that requires a spatial layout is better described with pictures than with words. Second, a large amount of the brain is devoted to visual processing, so sketching and interpreting drawings increases the involvement of those brain regions in idea generation. Third, it is often difficult to describe processes purely in words, so diagrams are helpful.[15]

One creative facilitation technique that uses drawing is brainwriting. Each person draws three ideas on a piece of paper and then passes it to the person next to them, to build on the ideas or generate new ones. Keep doing this until the paper comes back to its original author. In this way, everyone builds on everyone else's thoughts, without even talking. Be aware that it is sometimes difficult to interpret sketches, so it may be worth asking the participants to add some words next to their drawings.

Reverse brainstorming

Reverse brainstorming is a great solution for a group that has formed recently, is highly hierarchical, competitive or has high social anxiety. In this method, you ask the participants to come up with ideas in order to create the problem. You can ask, for example: 'How can we create the worst possible experience for our clients?', 'How can we make our organization less results-oriented?', 'How can our work as a group be less actionable?'

There is something liberating about trying to get it wrong. There is less social anxiety, as you are not looking for good ideas – quite the opposite. There is also guaranteed to be laughter. Laughter is always great when you want people to get creative. After you've listed all the bad ideas, you can usually spot a solution for your original problem.

What to do when the group is stuck

You may find yourself in a Develop meeting that is losing steam; the group feels stuck, or is in a creative rut. Here are some techniques you can have in your toolkit to rescue the situation.

List and challenge your assumptions

Ask the group: 'What are we assuming that has us stuck here?' Then have the group make a list. If there are many limiting assumptions, select the one that affects you the most. Then ask the group a simple question: 'Is this assumption true?' You will be surprised by how many times it isn't.

A common assumption that I have seen limiting many groups is the one that they need to come up with the solution themselves. Once you challenge this, they realize that they can ask others for help. Another common assumption is that they need to come up with the end result, while it is always possible to experiment and fine-tune later.

Brainstorm for questions

Another reason that you could be stuck is that you have not Defined the problem properly. I suggest you go back to the Define stage, and one way of doing this is by brainstorming for questions.

I used the brainstorming-for-questions technique with one of my clients. They were a big multinational company struggling with customer loyalty. I gave them four minutes in their subgroups to think up fifteen questions about the topic. Among the questions that people came up with was this one: 'Are we loyal to the customer?' This question framed the problem in a new and original way. Instead of the team looking for ways to make their customers more loyal to them, they decided to ideate on how they could become more loyal to the customer. This new angle created fresh ideas.

How to narrow down the ideas

You need to start narrowing down the ideas (converging) so you can select the best ones to move into the Decide stage. Use a physical or a virtual whiteboard and Post-it notes to re-arrange the ideas in space.

Start grouping similar ideas together. Resist the temptation to name the categories of ideas too early. Rearrange the ideas by relationship; only name the categories, if you feel you need to, towards the end. You can merge ideas, if they are similar, after you have received permission from the people who offered them.

Be careful not to use the words 'winning' or 'best' ideas. People attach their ego to their ideas, so we need to discard them in a gentle way. We do not want to create 'winners' or 'losers'. One way to narrow down the ideas is to place them on an 'effort versus impact' 2D matrix, which measures the **effort** required to implement the idea in terms of investment (time, energy or money) against the **impact** it would have on solving the problem.

Another way to evaluate ideas is by using IDEO's model.[16] IDEO evaluates the viability, feasibility and desirability of every idea.

- **Viability** is about how much the idea makes sense financially. Does it fit our budget? What is the expected return on investment? Is it aligned to our business goals?
- **Feasibility** refers to how easy it is to implement the idea. Do we have the technology necessary within reach? How long will the idea take to be implemented? Can the organization make it happen?
- **Desirability** is how much we like the idea. Does the idea fill a need? Does it fit into people's lives? Will it appeal to them? Will people want this?

You can also use a form of voting – for example, distributing a series of sticky dots among the ideas – to narrow down to the best ones. There are virtual tools that provide an easy way to implement 'dotmocracy' in remote meetings.

After you have narrowed down the ideas, you may want to move on to the Decide stage, or sometimes you will want to collect more data about the ideas. You may want to learn more about feasibility or cost. You may want to build a prototype and experiment. For an important decision, gathering more data can steer you in the right direction.

It is worth noting here that the group generating the ideas does not have to be the same group that decides the winning idea. Great ideas can come from the whole of the organization, and you want to tap into the collective creativity and imagination to solve meaningful problems. That said, wide groups may not have the big-picture view needed to evaluate the ideas effectively. The group may select a winning idea, only to find the real decision makers go with a different one. In this case, it is better to finish your Develop meeting on a high. Thank the group for their ideas and let them know when they should expect to hear about the idea that will move forward. Then set up a Decide meeting with the group that is more equipped to make the decision.

Summary

When we have an important problem to solve, spending time developing ideas rather than moving on with one or two obvious options will pay off. Table 2 summarizes the techniques we have discussed in this chapter.

More important than all the techniques is for you, as the meeting leader, to be really open to the ideas the team will come up with. Be willing to embrace the unexpected.

Once you have a good list of ideas, you can then start convergent thinking. Organize and potentially narrow down your

| Table 2: The Develop Ideas Stage

Create the conditions for creativity in your meetings	How to facilitate group ideation	What to do when the group is stuck
Embrace divergent thinking Adopt a 'yes, and' attitude Be comfortable with inefficiency and uncertainty Steer clear of hierarchies	Come up with ideas individually first and then use small groups Make ideas tangible Reverse brainstorming	List and challenge your assumptions Brainstorm for questions

ideas. Check whether you need to collect data; test and experiment with your options. When you have Developed the ideas, the next step is to Decide on a way forward.

5 Decide the Way Forward

Companies take millions of decisions every single day, and these decisions make or break them. However, 72 per cent of leaders think bad strategic decisions are as frequent as good ones, or even the prevailing norm in their organizations.[1] We know from experience that most company decisions fail to produce the desired results. More than 70 per cent of new manufacturing plants in North America, for example, close within their first decade of operation. Approximately three-quarters of mergers and acquisitions never pay off. And efforts to enter new markets fare no better; the vast majority end up being abandoned within a few years.[2] Bad decisions along with failures in execution are more common than we would like.

How do we make better strategic decisions? For starters, we get a group to work on the decision rather than an individual. According to Cloverpop's business decision database, a diverse team will make better decisions than an individual up to 87 per cent of the time.[3] Decide meetings are where we bring this diverse team together to make a decision.

You do not need a meeting for every decision – that would be a nightmare – but you will most probably need a meeting for the important decisions. These are the ones that Amazon's CEO Jeff Bezos calls 'one-way doors', as they will be difficult to draw back from. In this chapter, we will review the different group decision-making processes, we will learn how to avoid common decision-making traps, and we will explore how you can stir up productive conflict in your Decide meetings.

How you make group decisions

Imagine you are the chairman of the board and you deliberate about making an acquisition. Four members are against the acquisition while five members, including yourself and the CEO, want to do it. How would you make the decision? Would you say that this is a big bet for the company so if not everyone is on board, you won't go forward? Would you follow what the majority wants, and therefore go ahead with the acquisition? Will you delegate the decision to the CEO, judging that he is the expert, given that he has been working on this deal for the last few months? The decision-making process you choose is important. It will define whether you make the acquisition or not. McKinsey found that the quality of the decision-making process is six times more important than the quality of the analysis done for a specific decision.[4]

Let's have a look at the most popular decision-making processes: consensus, majority rule and consultative.

Consensus decision making
Consensus is when all the members of the group need to agree with a solution – or, as a minimum, accept that they can live with it. Consensus is more desirable when the potential harm of a bad decision is greater than the cost of missed opportunities. For example, consensus is often the go-to decision-making process for some venture capitalist funds; the partners all need to agree whether or not to invest in a company. Most

criminal-trial juries operate on a consensus basis; you would not want someone in jail if there is reasonable doubt about them being guilty.

The benefits of striving for consensus are that it forces participants to understand everyone's needs so that they can build a solution that satisfies all. During that process, the group can become more cohesive. It equalizes the power distribution in the group. When you earn the whole group's buy-in, you make it more likely that they will implement the solution.

That said, companies like Amazon or Google dislike consensus. It is slow and expensive, and it can lead to a lot of missed opportunities. The tech giants manage to sustain their pace of innovation because they do not strive for universal agreement.

It is worth noting here that culture plays a role. For example, while the USA is relatively egalitarian, American business decisions are mostly made top-down. In contrast, in Japanese or German culture people strive for consensus a lot more.[5] Bear these cultural preferences in mind when you lead a Decide meeting with an international team.

Consensus should be avoided for small decisions if you do not want to see your company's performance decline and your employees' frustration build up. Toy company Mattel made this mistake when their stock price started falling after 2010. Insiders attributed this to endless internal meetings where no decisions were made. Selecting a logo for a simple toy required eight meetings and twenty iterations. 'A 2013 redesign of one Mattel website involved nearly a year's worth of monthly meetings and hundreds of slides worth of decks,' according to one executive. 'By the time a decision was reached, the budget had already been reallocated to another project.'[6]

Striving for consensus can serve as a procrastination technique for difficult decisions. Individuals inside organizations who are terrified of making decisions can call meetings instead. Those meetings turn into more meetings, and the cycle is never-ending. It's the perfect crime; the decision maker gets to delay in a way that appears productive.

Consensus can also lead to lowest-common-denominator decisions. Participants may decide to compromise because they need to come to an agreement, but the final decision may not serve the group well. For example, imagine two managers who cannot agree on whom to promote from their team. So they decide to promote no one, as this is the only solution acceptable to both. They could end up losing a top-performing employee to the competition; definitely not the best outcome for the managers.

Consensus is not suitable when the group does not have enough information, or the trust in the group is low. It also does not work when there are no good options on the table and difficult decisions need to be made. In this situation it is a lot harder to get everyone to agree.

If you want to facilitate a consensus-building meeting, try giving a deadline. For example, you may say: 'If we can't come to an agreement by 5 p.m., I will ask Laura to make the decision.' Knowing that the decision will be taken away from the group can help people overcome minor disagreements.

When there is a good proposal on the table, ask: 'Who can't live with this?' If someone is opposed, this person has to show how the proposal can be made acceptable to them without making it worse for everyone else. Another useful question is: 'What would it take to get you on board?'

Majority-rule decision making

With majority-rule decision making you end up with some type of voting, and the majority decides. You may require a

50 per cent majority or a two-thirds majority. For majority rule to work well, the options need to be clear cut, and the team needs to be well informed.

The benefit of majority-rule decision making is that it is more likely to be perceived as democratic and fair. It increases the legitimacy of the decision, as it communicates that the majority liked the proposal. It can also lead to a firm decision being taken quickly.

Disadvantages include that it puts the emphasis on winning rather than coming up with the best decision. It might create politics, as people try to build alliances before the meeting so that they can win the majority vote. It also gives everyone's opinion the same weight, whether they are an expert or not.

Some managers are uncomfortable with conflict. They jump quickly to a vote, without giving an opportunity for people to try to reconcile the different opinions and create a new proposal. One of the biggest disadvantages of majority rule is that it can create an unhappy minority that sabotages the execution of the decision it did not vote for.

Here are some tips for effective facilitation of a majority-rule Decide meeting.

- **Have people vote individually and in writing first**. You do not want participants to be influenced by one another. It has been demonstrated that it is extremely difficult to disagree with the opinions of the people who spoke before you.[7] You can ask participants to write their vote on a Post-it and then share all the Post-its at the same time; or use one of the many online voting tools.
- **Make the voting anonymous**. This helps people to vote for what they believe, without caring too much about what their colleagues will think of them.

- **Get more information from participants than simply their first preference**. For example, you can give people a number of votes to distribute among various solutions. Rather than having people vote yes or no to a proposal, ask them to evaluate it using certain criteria. This method improves the quality of the decision making. You can ask people to rank the proposals in order of preference, and use an online tool to compute the group's overall ranking. You can have several voting rounds as you narrow down the number of options.

Consultative decision making

In consultative decision making, there is a clear decision owner. This decision owner will consult with the group in the meeting, whose role is to advise and influence, but in the end, she will make the final call. By having clear accountability, you increase your chances that a decision will be made. By having one person make the final call, the business can move fast.

The drawback of this decision-making method is that the group may hesitate to share their true opinion and may say what the leader of the group wants to hear. Consultants call this phenomenon the 'sunflower effect'. To counteract this, you need to encourage productive conflict (we will see how later in this chapter).

People who are consulted may think they have a vote and become frustrated when they realize that they don't. It is best to communicate who owns the decision, and how this decision will be made, at the beginning of a Decide meeting.

Jeff Bezos adopts a 'disagree and commit' principle. According to this principle, the aim is not to gain people's agreement (consensus) but rather their commitment to support the decision.

Here is an excerpt from Bezos' public letter to Amazon share-holders in 2016 that explains the principle.

> This phrase [disagree and commit] will save a lot of time. If you have conviction on a particular direction even though there's no consensus, it's helpful to say, 'Look, I know we disagree on this but will you gamble with me on it? Disagree and commit?' By the time you're at this point, no one can know the answer for sure, and you'll probably get a quick yes.[8]

What is interesting about Bezos is that he not only expects his team to disagree and commit with his views, but he says that he disagrees and commits all the time with decisions his team feel passionate about. For example, he did not agree with making a certain show for Amazon Prime but he wrote to his team that he hoped it would become the most watched thing they had ever made, thereby personally demonstrating the principle of 'disagree and commit'. Amazon can move a lot faster because they do not have to waste time convincing everyone. They just have to gain their commitment.

I have seen this principle work successfully in smaller com-panies, but it requires a lot of internal work from everyone in the organization. Managers may struggle to support a decision made by the leaders of the company that they personally dis-agree with. They may feel it is dishonest to give their backing to a decision in front of their team while they do not agree with it. On the other hand, if they openly disagree, they may inad-vertently sabotage the success of the decision and the company. As a leader, you need to find the fine balance: while it is best to openly disagree during the Decide meeting, once the decision is made, the most productive thing is usually to commit to it and support its success.

How you make sure the process is fair

There is no golden rule about which decision-making process is the best. It will depend on the nature of the decision and your company's culture. INSEAD professors Renée Mauborgne and Chan Kim found that employees will commit to a manager's decision – even one they disagree with – if they believe that the process the manager used to make the decision was fair.[9]

Fair process is not about consensus or democracy. It is about giving an opportunity for all ideas to be heard, and subsequently being clear on how a decision was made. CEOs often think their decision-making process is clearer than how their executives perceive it in reality.[10]

Now that you have selected a decision-making process, it is time to look at how you will increase the quality of your decisions.

Avoid group decision-making traps

If you want to improve the quality of your decision making in meetings, you will need to be aware of the most common biases and decision-making errors that afflict even the most diverse, inclusive groups. By helping to mitigate some of those biases, you can directly improve your company's bottom line, as a recent McKinsey study showed: when organizations worked at reducing the effect of bias on decisions about investments, their returns were up to seven percentage points higher.[11]

There are four common decision-making traps for groups. Let's take a look at each in turn.

Hidden profiles bias

Imagine that a hiring committee has to choose the right candidate for a marketing job. Objectively candidate A is a better candidate than B or C as she has a lot more skills, including copywriting, SEO, social media, design skills and more. Each member of the committee is aware of a different set of candidate A's skills. They have unique information. For candidates B and C, the committee members have more shared knowledge of the candidates' skills. They all know that candidate B is good in copywriting and SEO and candidate C in design and social media.

Almost always, this committee will choose the wrong candidate. They will fail to pool the unique information that the members have, which would inform them that candidate A is the best candidate. This experiment has been repeated many times, with the same terrible results.[12] The paradigm of failing to share unique information with the group is called the 'hidden profile'. One reason we may not bring up unique information is that we assume the others know it already. Also, we may feel uncomfortable bringing new information to a group as we want to help reach consensus. It feels safer to talk about common knowledge rather than disturbing the waters. And it is easier to forget information when we do not hear it again from our teammates. When there are hidden profiles in our meeting, we are eight times less likely to make the right decision.[13] It is important to encourage your meeting participants to share what they know.

Group polarization

Groups tend to make more extreme decisions than individuals would make. We become a lot more extreme in our positions when we see other people agreeing with us. For example, many boards will decide to pay more for an acquisition than the sum individual members had in mind before the meeting.[14] One of the reasons I recommended a secret vote in majority-rule decision making is to avoid polarization.

If you have two polarized groups in your meeting, ask them to switch sides and argue each other's position. Focus on creating understanding first and agreement second. Explore any psychological needs that are not being met. Participants in a polarized group may feel insecurity about their value in the organization, or perhaps a perceived lack of personal power is being relieved by forming a strong group that fights others.

Groupthink

Groupthink is a phenomenon where the group starts thinking with one mind. A symptom of groupthink is a perception of 'invulnerability'. Another symptom is closed-mindedness – rejecting any idea that challenges the group's assumptions. The group members also self-censor to maintain the consensus. Groups are particularly susceptible to groupthink when group members are similar in background and isolated from other sources of information.

The bombing of Pearl Harbor is attributed to groupthink.

Many of the officers at Pearl Harbor did not take warnings from Washington DC about potential invasion seriously despite the fact that Japanese messages had been intercepted. Those who didn't take action believed that the Japanese wouldn't dare to attempt an assault against the U.S. because they would recognize the futility of war with the United States.[15]

The bankruptcy of Swissair is also attributed to groupthink. The airline had so much money people called them 'the flying bank'. They thought they were invulnerable, leading to poor decisions and mismanagement.[16]

While polarization is about making more extreme decisions as a group than individuals themselves would make, groupthink results in a bad decision without anyone expressing dissenting views. Bringing in outside experts to consult on a decision can be one of the ways to mitigate groupthink.

Sunk cost fallacy

The sunk cost fallacy means that groups will tend to escalate their commitment to a losing strategy more than individuals would.[17] Indeed, behind most business failures you will find a leadership team clinging to a losing strategy.

HMV invested in new stores while people were shifting to buying CDs online. Nokia invested deeply in their own operating system, Symbian, while Apple's iOS and Google's Android were dominating the market. Kodak spent huge development and marketing budgets on film while the world had moved to digital photography.[18]

How to mine for productive conflict

You need to keep looking for the biases in your Decide meetings and calling them out. One of the most effective tools to do that – and to increase the quality of your group decisions – is productive conflict.

Think about your meetings. Do they have too much conflict or too little? Personal attacks in meetings create a toxic work environment and low performance. But so does the absence of conflict. With personal attacks, you have an unsafe, hostile environment where people blame each other and become territorial. With absence of conflict, the issues stay unresolved, and they are discussed in hallways or private chats. People do not feel they can raise dissenting views in the meeting.

Culture plays a role in how people perceive conflict in meetings. INSEAD professor Erin Meyer found that in some cultures you can reject an opinion without rejecting the person who suggested it, while in others this separation is more difficult. For example, in France, Greece or Germany you can have productive conflict without damaging the personal relationships, while this is more difficult in many Asian, Latin American and Arab countries.[19] The US and UK are right in the middle of the avoiding-confrontation continuum. What you want in your Decide meetings is healthy conflict that does not become personal, irrespective of the participants' cultural background.

If you sense the group is conflict-averse, emphasize how important it is to make a good decision. Given the uncertainty, you want to encourage diversity of thought and disagreements, even if this is uncomfortable. Different opinions will help the group surface and challenge their assumptions; this is a Decide meeting, and disagreement is encouraged. Try the following techniques.

Devil's advocates
You may have a person who naturally plays the role of the devil's advocate in the group. The way you treat this person is important; the other participants will observe your reaction as the leader of the meeting to see if it is OK to have an opposing view. When someone disagrees, say something like: 'Thank you, John, for bringing this new perspective. Who else shares

this view?' You could appoint a subgroup to try to find holes in the wider group's thinking, just like some companies pay hackers to try to hack into their systems.

Devil's advocates help mitigate group polarization, group-think and sunk cost fallacy as they challenge the group. If you are the one who wants to bring up a dissenting view in the meeting, try saying something like this: 'Let me play devil's advocate so we can explore both sides.' The group will be more open to listening to your dissenting views, without taking them personally.

Blind balance sheet

A great facilitation technique that works for important deci-sions is to draw a balance sheet. Have the group write down individually the pros and cons of every alternative. Then draw a joint balance sheet, where everyone shares the pros and cons they wrote, without identifying where they stand. Only after the balance sheet is complete and the group has had a chance to get a complete picture can it argue for its favourite option. Participants frequently change their mind during this process as more arguments and information come forward. This tech-nique can mitigate the hidden profiles bias, as everyone needs to share all the pros and cons they have at their disposal. Also, the blind balance sheet helps a group that avoids conflict bring all the different perspectives forward in a non-threatening way.

Gossiping technique

In the gossiping technique, the spokesperson for an idea pre-sents it to the group, and then the group has the task of criti-cizing and dissecting the idea. The presenter of the idea must observe this 'gossiping' silently. She may find it easier to turn her chair and back to the group and simply take notes. Or in a virtual environment turn off the camera and microphone. The group pretends the presenter is not there, and they proceed to knock down her argument without hesitation.

You can also use the gossiping technique to help people with a challenge they are facing. I was coaching a group of working parents on how to manage parenting and career successfully. I asked individuals to share their challenge and then turn around and hear the group gossiping about it. One father shared how his wife, who also worked, always complained about him not doing any school drop-offs and pick-ups. The group openly shared their opinions about how his wife was feeling, and how they thought he was partly responsible for the difficult situation. Due to the honest feedback he got, he was able to see the problem from a different perspective.

With the gossiping technique, people enrich their thinking and learn not to take criticism personally, as you create an artificially critical environment.

Pre-mortem

With a pre-mortem, you invite the group to think in advance about what could go wrong with their decision. The term 'pre-mortem' was coined by psychologist Gary Klein.[20] At a point when a management team had almost come to an important decision, but was not yet formally committed, he would say: 'Imagine that we are a year into the future. We implemented the plan as it now exists. The outcome was a disaster. Please write a brief history of that disaster.'

Participants who were prompted to apply prospective hindsight to a course of action came up with about 25 per cent more ways it could fail than those presented with an exercise in forecasting – and the reasons surfaced through prospective hindsight tended to be more specific and relevant to the situation.[21] The pre-mortem will help avoid polarization and groupthink by surfacing any dissenting views towards the decision made by the group.

Feedback exercise

If you have a group that works closely together but avoids candour and conflict, you can benefit by doing an exercise in which participants give feedback to each other. It is uncomfortable, but it strengthens the muscle for having honest discussions.

> **Step 1:** Participants write in their notebooks feedback about each person in the team. For each person, they write two or three of their behaviours that contribute to the strength of the team. They also write one of their behaviours that detracts from the strength of the team.

> **Step 2:** After everyone has finished writing, each person gets to hear everyone's feedback, silently taking notes, and in the end, they can comment on it.

The language you use when giving feedback is important. We need behaviours rather than personality characteristics. Neuroscience has proven that successful teams hear five compliments for every negative comment.[22] That is why it is important, depending on the time you have for the exercise, to ask people to share more positives than negatives. The groups I have done this exercise with have told me that it transformed the way they worked with each other and helped them deal with crises and difficult decisions more effectively.

Reduce toxic personal conflict

Successful teams feel comfortable sharing dissenting views, but what do you do when the conflict in your meetings turns personal and nasty? It is OK to have emotions during your meetings. That means you care. It is not OK to attack your colleagues personally. That is unprofessional. Here are some strategies that will help you to ensure that your meetings stay in the productive conflict area without getting toxic.

Bring data and facts

Work with data and facts when you make decisions. This way, you will avoid a lot of unnecessary conflict about personal opinions. When there is no data, people can start doubting each other's motives.

Google is a company with a huge data-driven culture. For example, they needed at a certain point to decide what shade of blue they should use for the links on the Google search page. Another company might have gone with voting or the opinion of the leader. Google made an experiment and tested 41 different shades of blue on 1 per cent of their audience. They found that the purple blue was clicked more often than the greenish blue. In Google's scale of business this meant an extra $200 million a year.

Provide the necessary data when you present something. Bring facts to your meetings. Build prototypes and experiment. You are bound to have less wasteful conflict.

Have many alternatives

When you debate only one or two options, it's easy for the conflict to turn personal. You have 'winners' and 'losers' – and as the opposing sides debate, their positions harden. When you spend time in the Develop stage to widen your options, you can vary the degree of support for different alternatives. People can change positions, with less risk of losing face by joining an 'opposite camp'.

Align on the decision-making criteria

Professor Peter Hawkins told me a story about a time when he was chairing the board of a company. In one of their meetings, the board got stuck arguing about whether to go ahead with an acquisition. What usually happens with these types of decisions is that either the group polarizes around two opposite views, or they get to groupthink and there is a debate but no generative dialogue.

According to Professor Hawkins, most of the dysfunction happens because people use different criteria to judge the decision. Some may say they do not agree because it is expensive, others because they do not have the bandwidth for implementation, while someone else may support the acquisition because it is a great culture fit. Professor Hawkins asked the group to write down the criteria they thought were important in judging a possible acquisition. Then they created a list of criteria on a flip-chart. The board members were each assigned five dots as votes to distribute among the criteria they considered most important. In less than twenty minutes the board had drawn up a list of criteria and reached alignment about what mattered. The CEO then went back and did their due diligence on these criteria. In the next board meeting, the decision was obvious to all.

Be aware of systemic tensions

I was coaching a team where the head of Sales was in conflict with the head of Customer Success. They each blamed the other for not doing their job properly. The Sales team would bring clients and turn them over to Customer Success. If the clients left in the first month, the Sales team would not make their commission, while there was no penalty for the Customer Success team. As many clients were dropping out during the first month, the conflict escalated. Sales blamed Customer Success for being lazy and not fighting to keep the clients. Customer Success blamed Sales overpromising as the reason the clients were leaving.

What seemed like a personal conflict was, in reality, a problem of misaligned incentives: the Customer Success team, as well as the Sales team, needed an incentive to keep the customer in their first month. Once the incentives were more aligned, the personal conflicts disappeared.

The incentives in companies are rarely aligned. That's why you have conflicts between PR and Compliance, Operations and Sales, and so on. By raising awareness of the systemic issues, you can help the individuals understand that the issue is not personal, and they can then work together to try to solve it.

Another form of systemic tension is an unbalanced power structure. When the leader is too autocratic, there is more interpersonal conflict. Lack of power and autonomy produce tension among the members of teams. When the leader is too weak, there is also more unproductive conflict, as the team members compete to fill the power vacuum. You need a balanced power structure, where people feel they have power and influence, but the leader acts as a natural tiebreaker.

Adopt non-violent communication

Microsoft CEO Satya Nadella bought all the members of his senior leadership team a copy of the book *Nonviolent Communication* by Marshall Rosenberg,[23] when he joined the company in 2014. There is plenty of research that proves the non-violent communication model is effective in rooting out the most unproductive elements of workplace conflict. Here it is in a nutshell (you can read Rosenberg's book to go deeper into the topic).

Step 1: Separate observation from judgement. Only share the facts: what you have observed and know to be true. For example, you may say: 'I have heard you supporting this strategy.' This way, people are less likely to perceive what you say as criticism.

Step 2: Share how you feel and which unmet need causes that feeling. There are four core feelings: joy, sadness, anger and fear. Sharing and naming your feelings, and linking them to your unmet needs, will help others understand you. They will be more likely to help you if you say something like: 'I feel angry considering this option, because I value the autonomy of my department.' Or 'I feel afraid considering this option, because I value security for the cashflow of the company.' When you hear someone talking in an emotional way, try to understand their unmet need.

Step 3: Make a request, without demanding, for example: 'Will you be willing to . . .?'

Humour is crucial in promoting healthy conflict in groups.[24] Encourage humour by bringing it in as a leader. By creating social time outside the meeting, you will also see more humour in your meetings.

For more ideas about leveraging humour in your meetings, business and life in general, take a look at the book *Humour, Seriously* by Jennifer Aaker and Naomi Bagdonas.[25]

Adopting the language patterns of non-violent communication, and bringing in the humour, will improve the quality of your meetings.

Eliminate toxic behaviours

Another strategy I have found helpful when working with teams is raising awareness about the toxic behaviours they display in their meetings. There are four toxic behaviours that manifest in relationships and teams:

- blame
- defensiveness
- stonewalling, and
- sarcasm.

They were dubbed the 'Four Horsemen of the Apocalypse' by Dr John Gottman when he was researching what causes marriages to fail.[26] These four horsemen will cause your meetings to fail as well.

Try this exercise in your next meeting to raise awareness of any toxic behaviours. Write each one of the four toxic behaviours on four big pieces of paper. Then put the pieces of paper in four separate corners of the room. Ask the group to stand up and walk towards the toxic behaviour that is most prominent in the group. With this constellation, you create awareness about what toxic behaviour exists, without anyone needing to say a word.

Then ask people to walk towards the toxic behaviour that they exhibit most often when they have a bad day. We can all default to any of these behaviours when we are at our worst. Once participants have seen how they contribute to any toxicity in the environment, you can have a discussion about how to eliminate the toxins from your meetings. You can adapt this exercise to a virtual meeting by using one of the white-board tools and voting. One leadership team I worked with found this exercise so useful that they replicated it with their own teams. After this exercise, it becomes easier to call out the toxins if you see them occur in your meetings. A question I love to use is: 'Are we willing to solve this without blame?'

Creating an environment that nurtures productive conflict is important. Meetings are the best place to build an honest, open culture for your company while avoiding toxicity.

Summary

Good decisions matter. Bain Consultancy found a '95 per cent correlation between companies that excel at making and executing key decisions and those with top-tier financial results, whether measured in terms of revenue growth, return on capital or total shareholder return'.[27] In this chapter, we have looked at ways to maximize the chances of success when you hold Decide meetings. Table 3 summarizes how to make group decisions, and how to avoid the most common decision-making traps.

| Table 3: The Decide Stage

How you make group decisions	Avoid group decision-making traps
Consensus decision making	Hidden profiles bias
Majority-rule decision making	Group polarization
Consultative decision making	Groupthink
	Sunk cost fallacy

Ensure a fair process, which means listening to people and explaining how the decision was made and what you expect from them. It is crucial that you mine for productive conflict that does not get personal. Table 4 summarizes the things you can do to build a productive conflict culture in your meetings.

Once you have a clear decision, you will be able to move on to the Do stage, which is about implementation.

| Table 4: Mine for Productive Conflict in Your Meetings

Techniques to increase productive conflict	How to reduce toxic personal conflict
Devil's advocates	Bring data and facts
Blind balance sheet	Have many alternatives
Gossiping technique	Align on the decision-making criteria
Pre-mortem	Be aware of systemic tensions
Feedback exercise	Adopt non-violent communication
	Eliminate toxic behaviours

6 Do! Execute, Plan and Inspire for Action

In the Do meeting (or stage) the outcome is action, which may happen in the meeting or afterwards. A Do meeting is where you create change and make a difference. Unless you get people to implement your ideas and decisions, nothing changes.

There are three types of Do meetings:

- working sessions
- action-planning sessions, and
- inspire-action meetings.

Let's take a look at how you can make all three types of Do meetings successful.

How to have successful working sessions

In a working session, you collaborate to produce a piece of work during the meeting. The group is all together, working on a single problem, away from distractions. You can achieve extraordinary results in a very short time. You do not need much project management and you do not have to wait for asynchronous communication.

There are several types of working sessions. The most

common type is two or three people in front of a computer working on some type of product – whether this is a pitch deck, an ad campaign, or lines of code. In a remote environment it would be in front of a shared document or screen. Longer and more sophisticated working sessions are hackathons, war rooms and design sprints.

Hackathons

Hackathons usually produce product prototypes. They started in tech companies, with great success. Many of the Facebook products were first created during hackathons, including the Like button, Timeline and Chat. Looking at the hackathons' success, more companies adopted them and now over 80 per cent of Fortune 100 companies conduct hackathons to drive innovation.[1]

War rooms

In a war room, all the experts and decision makers are together and can move quickly. A war room could be useful during a crisis or during an important event. The first time I experienced a war room was when Procter & Gamble invited me as a Googler to join their 2012 Olympics War Room in Cincinnati. They had brought marketing experts and representatives from their key digital partners together in one room to be able to react quickly with their messaging to what was happening in the Olympic Games.

Design sprints

Design sprints originated at Google Ventures and are now adopted by thousands of companies around the world, in several adaptations. Originally, they were a five-day event with the objective to end up with a working prototype. The key difference between design sprints and hackathons is that in a design sprint the group selects a winning idea on Day Two and then everyone works on that, while in a hackathon you have multiple teams working on different ideas, and the best idea is selected at the end.

Giorgos Vareloglou is the co-founder of Reborrn, a company that runs design sprints for some of the largest companies in Europe. Among their achievements is helping Coca-Cola Austria launch a direct-to-consumer e-commerce platform in three days.[2] Vareloglou shared with me his best tips for running successful working sessions that produce results at breakneck speed. You need to have:

- an environment free of distractions
- the decision makers in the room (physical or virtual)
- your best talent in the room (physical or virtual)
- a clear definition of 'done', and
- tight time frames (so tight that you can't even call it a project – this makes asynchronous communication unnecessary).

How to have successful action-planning sessions

For longer and more complex projects, you will need to coordinate the work of several people over a period of time. In this case, you will probably need another type of Do meeting – the action-planning session – to get people aligned on how to move forward.

We know that good decisions are not enough. Many companies never manage to implement their good decisions. Their teams do not follow through, they get distracted or abandon the project. Even those who manage to execute the decision often find that their planning was way off the mark. The Sydney Opera House took ten years longer and cost almost fifteen times more than the forecast.[3] The Denver International Airport was completed sixteen months later than scheduled and cost $2 billion more than the planned budget.[4]

Scientists Dan Lovallo and Daniel Kahneman coined the term 'planning fallacy', which they defined as 'the tendency to underestimate the time, costs, and risks of future actions and at the same time overestimate the benefits of the same actions'.[5] Researchers found that the planning fallacy applied in 78 per cent of projects.[6] The planning fallacy is aggravated in groups, which are even more optimistic than individuals about the time and resources necessary to complete a task.[7] How can your action-planning meetings produce a solid plan that gets executed on time and within budget? Here are four strategies that will significantly increase the odds of your action-planning meeting being successful.

- Plan for obstacles.
- Break down the project into milestones.
- Learn from similar projects.
- Address the security needs of the people and departments you want to collaborate.

Plan for obstacles

Visualizing success and writing down potential obstacles increases the probability of successful implementation of your goals.[8] Once you get your meeting participants to write down the potential obstacles, engage in if-then planning. More than 200 studies have shown that if-then planners are about 300 per cent more likely to reach their goals.[9]

How do you implement if-then planning in your meeting? You need to decide what the triggers are and what the desired action should be. This is useful in planning how to deal with potential obstacles but also as a way to instil new behaviours and habits in your group.

Let's imagine that you want to increase communication across the team. Your plan could be something like this: **If** it is Friday 2 p.m., **then** we send an email with our updates to the team. You have a **trigger** (Friday 2 p.m.) and a **response** (send the email). In an experiment, the teams that implemented the if-then planning had only 90 minutes' delay in sending the email, while the control group who did not use if-then planning had eight hours' delay.[10] For an obstacle, you may say something like: 'If we do not deliver the product on time, then we reimburse the client the delivery cost.' Again, you have a trigger and a desired action.

What happens, though, with the obstacles that you cannot predict? Military leaders say that no plan survives contact with the enemy. Even more important than a detailed plan is to make sure that your intention is clear to everybody.

The implementation of a decision will usually require multiple additional decisions. Are there any general guidelines that you can give that will empower the group to make these decisions on their own and still make sure they are rowing in the same direction? French military leader Napoleon Bonaparte was the first to use this technique when he gave the guideline: 'March towards the sound of the guns.' Before then, when in battle, the troops either looked to their leader to see what they had to do, or they made the decision on their own, often contradicting one another. With the guideline 'march towards the sound of the guns' Napoleon ensured that, no matter what happened, the troops would know what to do.

Intel did something similar.[11] They created a rule that production capacity would be allocated to products according to certain criteria, prioritizing profit margin per wafer. When microprocessors started having higher margin per wafer than memory chips, the company redirected its production capacity towards microprocessors. Most top managers at the time were still committed to memory chips, but the guideline called for a different action than that which the managers wanted. The rule helped the company adapt quickly to the market and change their business successfully. How can you communicate your intention to the organization clearly and succinctly?

Break down the project into milestones

One of the proven ways to reduce the planning fallacy is to break the project down into milestones.[12] This way, you can better calculate the time and investment for each of those steps. Once you have agreed with your group on the milestones, you can use one of the many collaboration tools to track progress against them. The agile development methodology, which is a set of principles for teamwork, divides the work of complex projects into bite-sized pieces, which they call 'sprints'. The team plans a sprint, implements the sprint, reviews the work and also does a retrospective on what they should improve for their next sprint. By breaking a project into milestones, you can move faster and also better adapt to the environment.

Learn from similar projects

You can avoid planning fallacy by exploring similar projects; how long they took and how much they cost. Academics Dan Lovallo and Daniel Kahneman share an example of being part of an academic team that was developing a new curriculum for high schools in Israel.[13] When the participants were asked how long the project would take, they answered between eighteen and thirty months. Then they asked a curriculum expert how long similar projects had taken in the past. The expert shared that 40 per cent of similar teams gave up the project without ever completing it. The rest took, on average, seven years to complete the curriculum. The curriculum expert went on to say that Lovallo's and Kahneman's team was below average in resources and potential. The academic team ignored the expert and continued working on the project for more than eight years. The resulting curriculum was hardly ever used. Had they listened to the curriculum expert, they would have abandoned the project and saved a lot of time, money and frustration.

Address the security needs of the people and departments you want to collaborate

The Product and Marketing departments of a company I worked with needed to collaborate for the launch of a new financial product. The collaboration was not going smoothly. Marketing was pushing for a feature to be included for the launch, and Product did not agree. The departments started having separate meetings to plan the launch rather than joint ones. The information was not flowing freely between them. Things went south when Marketing booked some advertising on a date when the new product would not be ready. Nobody had informed them about the change in the product delivery schedule.

Collaboration initiatives often fail in companies. Researcher Lisa B. Kwan studied this phenomenon for years, trying to figure out why.[14] It was not evident: executives explained why collaboration was important, developed action plans, appointed a leader of the collaboration initiative, and they gave good funding. Still they found these initiatives failed, again and again:

departments would make important decisions on their own, and they would not share information.

Kwan finally identified the reason. When we ask one department to work with another, the department's sense of identity, legitimacy and control can be threatened. To collaborate effectively you may need to lose some control. You may also feel you are giving away part of your territory that supports your sense of identity and legitimacy as a useful department within the company. In the example above, the Product team felt threatened by Marketing dictating features; that was their job. If they gave away this decision to Marketing, then what was their role in the company?

How do you address the security needs of your departments or individuals before you ask them to collaborate? Be clear about what the role of each department is; it might have changed with the new initiative. Emphasize why each department is important and unique for the company. Consider granting the group greater ownership over other areas not associated with the collaboration initiative. This will make them more willing to give up some of their control in the area you need them to.

How to inspire action in your meetings

Let's take a look at the third type of Do meetings, the ones that have as their objective to move people. They can be a meeting of just two people, or a crowd of thousands. Think of the 'I have a dream' speech of Martin Luther King, for example. An inspiring meeting has the power to sell products, make millions, change lives or even shift the course of history. In business, you have meetings with the objective to inspire action all the time. Maybe you want to get funding for your idea. Close a deal with a big customer. Or get another department to adopt a new process. How do you inspire people effectively? Let's review some of the best strategies to move people into action in your meetings.

Understand your audience's motivations

You need to understand two things about your audience to be able to inspire them. What do they want? And what do they struggle with? The action you want them to take needs to help them achieve pleasure and avoid pain. Otherwise, they will not take it.

To answer the question about what your audience wants, I have found author Daniel Pink's motivation model helpful.[15] He argues that there are three intrinsic motivators:

- mastery (we need to feel competent at what we do)
- autonomy (we need to feel we have control over the how and what of our work), and
- meaning (we need to feel that our work matters).

Does what you want your meeting participants to do increase their mastery, autonomy or meaning? If yes, say so.

If people fund your project, for example, will they contribute to the world in a positive way, getting more meaning? Will they acquire more industry knowledge, achieving more mastery? Or, will they generate more revenue, and thus have more autonomy?

If you want to move people, you need to appeal to their emotions as well as their intellect. What is the pain your proposal alleviates? What fear will your solution ease out? What is an unfairness that makes you and your counterparts angry and is worth collaborating to fight against? People make important decisions emotionally and then they look for data to back them up.[16] This is not what we learned in our economics class but it is what countless studies have shown.

Do your research to understand your audience's wants and pains. By speaking to their internal motivation, it is more likely that they will take action.

Craft a simple, unexpected and concrete message

I was speaking to seventy Columbia and INSEAD alumni entrepreneurs in Paris. The two French alumni associations had partnered for the first time for this event, a workshop on how to be a successful entrepreneurial leader. This workshop was a Do meeting; I knew that stress and feeling overwhelmed were key obstacles to entrepreneurial success, and I wanted to convince entrepreneurs to do something about them.

I invited three volunteers to the stage. I pulled out one balloon and asked the first volunteer to keep the balloon up in the air. He could do it easily by tapping the balloon upwards. Then I added more balloons, and he needed to keep all of them in the air. He started struggling and then failing; the balloons were falling to the floor. I asked him to start over but this time to ask for help from the other two volunteers. The exercise became easy again and the three volunteers had fun keeping the balloons up in the air. I asked the volunteers and the audience what they had learned from the exercise. The message was simple: 'As an entrepreneur, you cannot keep all the balloons in the air alone. You will get stressed and fail. You need to ask for help.'

When Steve Jobs presented the iPod he said: 'One thousand songs in your pocket.' This is a message that is crafted masterfully. It is simple, visual and unexpected. How can you adopt these qualities in your message? Can you use images or props? Can you surprise your audience? Is your idea easy to understand?

Use the power of stories

One of the best ways to connect emotionally with your audience is to tell stories. We are wired for stories. We carry stories, share them, and love to hear them. In my coaching practice I use stories in two ways. First, I help the client explore their own stories and see if they need to be reshaped or reframed. Groups often get stuck because of the stories they tell themselves, and old stories may hinder them from taking action in a meeting.

If the group has made a wrong decision in the past, they may build a wall against new ideas from fear of something similar happening. Maybe a client has been burned in the past by working with a supplier in your industry. You need to hear that story, to show how the current situation is different. Maybe your direct report resists your authority because he had a bad experience with a previous boss. Hearing that story, and helping reframe it, can facilitate a behavioural change. How can you review the stories your meeting counterparts have? Is there a need to reframe them to get them unstuck?

The second way I use stories in my coaching practice is by sharing stories, mine or others'. Stories provide a sense that you are not alone and that there is light at the end of the tunnel. Other people have gone through similar situations and have emerged on the other side, stronger and wiser. You can transform your Do meetings by using stories to demonstrate empathy and provide inspiration. If it is a sales meeting, share how you helped another client achieve their goals. If it is a speech, share a personal story to show your audience that you have been in their shoes.

Close by respecting your counterparts' free will

One of the most challenging stages of inspire-action meetings is the closure. This is when you ask for the deal or tell your counterparts to take action. There is conflicting advice about how to do this. What is certain is that if you have built trust throughout your meeting, people will be more open to what you have to say during the closing stage. Nobody likes to feel pushed or manipulated.

Former FBI hostage negotiator Chris Voss argues that people in a negotiation setting find it easier to say no than yes. He suggests you frame your closing question in such a way that your desired answer is no. For example: 'Would it be a crazy idea to fund this project with two million dollars?' If you have done your job of influencing well, the other party will say: 'No, it is not a crazy idea.' A salesperson could say: 'Is there any reason why we can't proceed with the shipment?'

This idea is contrary to many other negotiation techniques, one of which recommends that you ask the prospective client whether they would like the car in blue or red even before they have said they are going to buy it. Closing with a 'no question' feels more genuine. However, you will need to adopt language that feels authentic to you, otherwise you risk making your counterparts feel manipulated.

Summary

Remember that the outcome of Do meetings is action. By inspiring action in your meetings, you create the impact you want to have in the world.

Table 5 summarizes the best practices we have looked at in this chapter, to make sure your Do meetings are a success.

Congratulations, you now have a good understanding of how you can best achieve your meeting's Purpose. The 4D Meeting Framework helps you identify the desired outcome(s)

| Table 5: The Do Outcome

Working sessions	Action-planning sessions	Inspire-action sessions
A distraction-free environment	Plan for obstacles	Understand your audience's motivations
Decision makers and best talent in the room	Use milestones	
	Learn from similar projects	Craft a simple, unexpected and concrete message
A clear definition of 'done'	Address security needs of the people involved	Use the power of stories
Tight time frames		Close by respecting your counterparts' free will

for your meeting and structure it accordingly. If you have not yet reviewed your calendar to categorize your meetings with regard to the 4Ds, now is a good time to do it. I also encourage you to consolidate your learning by writing down your top three takeaways from the first part of the book. What is it that you will do differently from now on because of what you have read in Part One?

PART TWO

People and Process

In Part One, we looked at the Purpose of your meeting. The skills you have learned through the 4D Meeting Framework will not only help you run more successful meetings but also make you a more impactful leader overall. Taking care of the People and the Process of your meetings will take it all to the next level.

In Part Two, we will go deeper into how to make your 4D meeting a success. We will look at key strategies for nurturing the People in your meetings and making sure you get their best contributions. We will then explore Process and identify easy fixes you can adopt to make sure your meetings and working days are set up for success.

| Figure 3: Purpose, People and Process Triangle

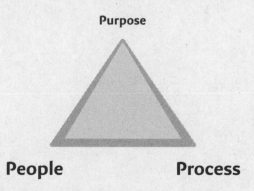

7   Connect with Others

A meeting, at the end of the day, is an act of love. You bring people together to work towards a better future. You need to take care of yourself first, to be able to serve others. You cannot give from an empty cup. That is especially true when you want to hold successful meetings.

We will start this chapter with how you can nurture yourself so that you show up at your best in meetings. Then we will explore how you can best connect with others. Finally, we will close this chapter by covering two special formats of 4D meetings: the one-to-ones with your direct reports, and the all-hands.

How to nurture and connect with yourself

It was October 2015, and this day was going to be one of the most embarrassing of my career. I was still an employee at Google and I was running a one-day meeting with all the European CEOs of my agency client. I had organized the whole thing, coordinated the speakers, and I was a host and a speaker myself. My manager and my whole team were coming from the US to London for the event. The president of our organization happened to also be in London that week and I had secured him as a keynote speaker. I was excited!

At the time, I had a small baby. Before the big day, I did not sleep at all – a combination of baby duties and stress. Everything was going smoothly at the event, until the moment I stood up to introduce our president. As I started doing that, my mind went blank. I was not sure about his surname. I had worked with another colleague that week who shared the same first name, and I felt I was mixing up their surnames. So I said the president's first name and then I took a long (well, it seemed like a century to me) pause while trying to think. I decided not to take the risk of saying the wrong surname, so I said nothing. I awkwardly asked the president to come to the stage. Embarrassed, I sat down.

Sleep deprivation impairs memory and cognitive performance. I had put all this work into that meeting, but because I had neglected my self-care, I failed to perform in the way I wanted. If you are to hold successful meetings, you need to take care of yourself first. You want to walk into the meeting feeling energetic, confident, centred. How you show up will have a tremendous impact on how good a job you will do. Good energy is contagious. And we also know that positivity boosts creativity and performance.[1] By taking care of yourself first, you take care of your participants and your meeting.

Here are some tips on how to best put yourself into a positive state for your meeting.

Take care of your body
Sleep, hydrate, eat healthy food and move. We underestimate how taking care of our body influences our cognitive and social performance. Prioritizing your well-being can have more impact on the success of your meeting than a few extra hours of preparation.

Take care of your mind

Nerves are normal in big meetings, but they can sabotage you. We tend to want to get away from overwhelmed people. Exactly when you need people to connect with you, your nervousness can push them away. Think about how difficult it is to laugh at the jokes of a stand-up comedian who looks nervous, even if the jokes are good.

However, pushing away or ignoring your fear is not the solution. You are better off acknowledging it and allowing it to exist. Take a pause before your meeting and recognize your feelings. Try to investigate the sensations they cause in your body. Where in your body do you feel the fear and anxiety? What does that part of you need? Maybe some encouragement? Maybe a reminder that, whatever happens in the meeting, you will be OK?

It is important to support your mental well-being before your meeting. You can put on inspiring music. Maybe watch an empowering video. Meditation or a relaxing podcast can help. Visualize yourself doing a great job at your meeting. Try to get in contact with nature. A walk in the park to breathe fresh air before the meeting starts will help.

When my daughter went to a new school, I would give her a small toy to put in her pocket and tell her that I had poured my love into it. Whenever she felt lonely or scared, she could touch it and feel my love. This worked, and now she has started doing the same with me when I have important meetings. She gives me a small toy for 'luck'. The toy has a similar effect on me as it had for my daughter. If there is a difficult point in the meeting, I can look at the toy or touch it and immediately remember my daughter's love. I have since found out that oxytocin, the hormone of love, can help alleviate anxiety.[2] So, too, does focusing on your senses. You can develop some tricks to keep yourself grounded when you are too nervous or emotional in your meetings. Use an artefact or an image as an anchor, like I do. Alternatively, bring your attention into your body, feel your breathing, or your feet touching the floor. After having taken care of your body and mind, you will then be ready to connect with others.

How to connect with others

We connect with people we find likeable and credible. We have been programmed to judge these two dimensions through evolution. Millennia ago, when someone from outside our tribe approached us suggesting something, we would ask ourselves two questions: is this person a friend or a foe? Is this person capable of doing what they say they want to do? We still reflect on these questions today when we meet someone, although maybe in a slightly different manner: Does this person have good intentions? Does this person know what they are talking about?

Building rapport as well as boosting our likeability and credibility are important for holding successful meetings. We can do that by showing empathy, authenticity, appreciation and authority.

Empathy

In the previous chapter we talked about how important it is to understand where your fellow participants stand. What does your counterpart want, and what is their pain? How does it feel to be them? How does the world look through their eyes?

Show your counterparts that you care about their goals and

challenges and their points of view. Theodore Roosevelt was on to something when he said: 'People do not care how much you know, until they know how much you care.' Share if you have been in their shoes, or if you have helped other people with the same problem. Be careful not to become carried away with constantly talking about you, as this may stand in the way of building a real connection.

People are more likely to like you if you establish common ground. What do you have in common with them? Look for similarities – maybe schools, cities, people you both know – and refer to them early on. We like people who are like us. There is plenty of research suggesting that mirroring the other person's body language helps build more rapport. We do it subconsciously when we try to connect – and it works.[3]

Paying attention during your conversations will instantly make you appear more charismatic and allow you to connect more deeply with others. Oprah Winfrey built a meteoric career founded on her ability to be completely present with her interviewees. Practise active listening, which means listening to understand rather than listening to prepare your response. Show that you have listened by reflecting back what people have said, summarizing or paraphrasing.

Authenticity

To do business with you, people need to trust you. To build trust, you need to show up authentically in your meetings. Being authentic does not mean you need to reveal everything about yourself. It means not pretending you are someone else.

Many of my coaching clients have learned for years to suppress their emotions at work to appear professional. Sometimes this backfires, as they become robotic in their communications, failing to inspire other people. Let's not forget that most of our decisions are made emotionally, and by trying to eradicate emotion from our conversations, we are missing out. If you are passionate or enthusiastic about something, show it. If you are sad or frustrated, you can also communicate it in a professional way. Your influence will increase if you show up at your meetings as a human being rather than a machine.

Appreciation

It is easy to be judgemental of others. Judging people as enemies, or incompetent, is an evolutionary trait that once ensured our survival. Nowadays, we often believe that we can do a better job than our boss, and that our client does not really 'get it'.

Many studies have demonstrated that a whopping 70 to 90 per cent of participants believe they are better than average.[4] It does not matter what the topic is. The results are the same whether people are asked about their driving, teaching, or other skills. And while this overconfidence can be useful for selling and influencing, it will sabotage us if it comes across as arrogance. If we approach our meeting with an air of superiority, the other participants will tend to dislike us and therefore resist our message.

Going into a meeting thinking we are smarter than the other attendees is counterproductive. Go in with respect and appreciation. Search for things to value and appreciate in your colleagues. If they say something that does not make sense to you, rather than jump to the conclusion that they are ill intentioned, or incompetent, get curious. What they said makes sense to them, so there must be a piece of information you're missing. Ask many questions. By doing that, you will realize that what seemed outrageous in the beginning ceases to be so, once you see the full picture.

How to build authority in your meeting

It is not enough to be likeable for people to listen to you in your meetings. You need to be credible as well. People need to believe that you know what you are doing. Do not wait until the meeting starts to establish your authority. Do it beforehand, if you can. Can you find someone to introduce you or vouch for you? Can you send credibility-boosting information before the meeting?

I learned this the hard way when I had a meeting with an HR director to sell my coaching services. A common contact had introduced us. I wrongly assumed he would have looked me up on the internet. In the meeting I focused more on likeability and tried to establish a connection. I did not want to boast about my achievements. As a result, the HR director got the impression – mainly driven by my young appearance – that I was inexperienced. When clients in his firm wanted to hire me as a coach, he opposed it. This could have been avoided if I had established my credibility with a simple email before the meeting, sharing some of my achievements.

Don't make the same mistake. Send an email along these lines: 'I am looking forward to meeting you. Here are some parts of my experience that I believe will be relevant to our discussion.' Or a simple one-liner: 'You can read my bio below.'

In the meeting itself, choose your introduction wisely. You can boost your credibility by sharing third-party testimonials, case studies and facts, rather than boasting about yourself, as that will have the opposite effect. I remember when I was in account management, I used to introduce myself by saying: 'I look after that client.' Even though I managed an account that contributed a billion dollars to my company, nobody would have known by the way I was introducing myself. I made a slight change in words, saying: 'I run the partnership with that client.' I provided some facts, where appropriate, and people's perception of my seniority changed.

Choose your words wisely

The language we use is an important medium to establish our credibility. Avoid apologetic language, verbal tricks and filler words. Here is a selection of words and phrases that can detract from your credibility:

- actually
- really
- like
- you know
- just
- to be honest
- know what I mean
- very
- anyway
- basically
- literally
- sort of
- kind of
- this might be a stupid question.

Adopt a conversational speed

The pace with which you speak will influence your authority. Sometimes, when we don't feel confident, we speak quickly. We want to get it over with, or we do not want to take up too much time. You want to have a conversational speed that slows down for important points and speeds up during anecdotes and stories. Allow for pauses, to make sure the message lands and people have enough time to process it, but also do not be so slow that people get bored.

Get to the point

Rambling too much decreases our authority. Get to the gist of your argument quickly, and then pause and wait for people to react. Do not beat around the bush or keep repeating the same point. Earlier in my career, I got the feedback that I was repeating myself too much in conference calls. As I could not see the body language of the other participants, and I did not hear any verbal confirmations, I assumed they had not understood what I said, and so I kept repeating it. After I got the feedback, I learned to state my point and then ask for the participants' response.

The clearer the point you are making, the more effective you will be in establishing your authority. Some people believe that by using jargon, or complex language, they appear as experts, but the opposite is true. If you can explain something simply, you will be perceived as more of an expert.

Own your space

Our body language is crucial to how other people perceive us. Many of us will lose authority by trying to take up minimal space. We will drop our shoulders, cross our arms and legs, try to become tiny. To increase authority in meetings, you need to stand up tall and have an 'open' body language. For example, showing the palms of your hands can subconsciously inspire trust. In a virtual meeting, you would need to gesticulate in the field the camera captures to be able to show your hand movements. Eye contact is also important. During an in-person meeting, look one participant in the eyes, and change participants every time you finish a point. For a virtual meeting, position the camera close to where you see the participants in your screen. Avoid looking too much at your notes, your slides or at empty space.

Project your voice

Voice is another factor that impacts our authority. Most of us were born having a strong voice; you can hear it if you go outside any primary school or nursery. Kids are loud. But during our childhood we were told repeatedly not to shout too much. As a result, we do not project our voice enough to be effective in our meetings and presentations. Actors, singers and professional speakers exercise their voice on a daily basis, because it matters for effective communication. If you often have virtual meetings, invest in a good microphone, it will make all the difference.

Warren Buffett said that taking a speaking course when he was young was one of the best investments he ever made.[5] If working with a speech coach or joining a toastmasters' group feels too much, there are now apps where you can record your speech and get feedback on voice, pace, facial expressions, use of filler words, and more.

One-to-one meetings with your direct reports

Let's now look at how you can connect in a special breed of 4D meeting that is especially important for your work: one-to-one meetings with your direct reports. While you want to establish open communication and trust in your team meetings, one-to-one meetings are equally important. One-to-ones are where you discuss topics that are not relevant to the whole team, as well as topics that your direct report may not yet feel comfortable bringing up in front of the rest of their colleagues.

Venture capitalist and author Ben Horowitz argues that:

> The key to a good one-on-one meeting is the understanding that it is the *employee's* meeting rather than the manager's meeting. This is the free-form meeting for all the pressing issues, brilliant ideas and chronic frustrations that do not fit neatly into status reports, email and other less personal and intimate mechanisms.[6]

Most one-to-ones are Define meetings, but they can span all the 4Ds. In one-to-one conversations you have the opportunity to build deeper connections, handle personal topics, coach, and gain access to unique information. Here are some of the key topics to cover with your direct reports in your one-to-ones.

- What success looks like for the company, their work and themselves personally
- What is working well and what isn't
- Where they need your help
- What feedback they have for you

Before you get into all of those strategic questions, I suggest you start your meeting with a simple 'How are you?' A one-to-one meeting is the best place to learn about your employees' well-being and mental health. One of my coaching clients, a CEO in a multinational company, had a very difficult one-to-one with a talented team member who was not progressing well. When they talked about performance, she completely collapsed and revealed she had serious family issues. He said: 'I am so sorry . . . I didn't know what you were going through!

Why didn't you tell me?' 'You never asked me how I was doing . . .' she answered. Since then, he always starts his one-to-ones with the simple question: 'How are you?' He argues that it does wonders when you mean it.

Ask your direct report to send you the agenda beforehand. This makes it clear that it is her meeting, and she can also cancel if there is nothing to discuss. The one-to-one is an important meeting for your report and also for you. Commit to a frequency for your one-to-ones, and do not cancel them. As a manager, being there for your direct reports is one of the most important jobs you have. By frequently cancelling, you send the message that your management responsibilities are low on your list of priorities. Your direct report might have been waiting days for this meeting, and it can be disheartening to face a cancellation.

Avoid the advice trap in these meetings. If your direct reports are competent and experienced, you will want to withhold advice and try to coach them instead on whatever issue they are having. Ask them what they suggest should be done. Then ask them more questions, to help them think. It might look like more work in the short term, as it may be quicker just to tell them what to do. But it will save you time in the long run when your direct reports learn to deal with more issues on their own.

Facebook executive Julie Zhuo shares this tip: 'Strive for all your one-on-one meetings to feel a little awkward. Why? Because the most important and meaningful conversations have that characteristic.'[7] Discussing mistakes, fears, aspirations is not easy, but it is essential for your relationships with your team members.

All-hands meetings to inspire action and shape culture

All-hands meetings (also known as 'town halls') are the ones you have with your whole organization, and they can be expensive. Take the BBC, for example, an organization that has a famous meetings culture. It has 23,000 employees and an average salary of £40,000, so an all-hands meeting lasting one hour costs half a million pounds. For a bigger company with a higher average salary – like Facebook – a one-hour all-hands meeting can cost more than $3 million.

The biggest mistake leaders make is that they do not realize that the all-hands is a Do meeting. They squander thousands of employee hours going through boring slide decks and updates. All-hands are not about informing, even if they have information. They are about inspiring employees. They are about helping them to feel more emotionally connected to the company and its purpose. Successful all-hands meetings can encourage employees to stay with the company longer, to be an advocate for their employer, and to go the extra mile in their work. Once you are clear that all-hands are there to inspire action, you can set yourself up for success.

How can you use your all-hands meetings to appeal emotionally to your employees, shape your culture and inspire? Treat them as the important production that they are. Prepare, prepare, prepare. Analyse your audience. Build on your likeability by establishing common ground. Craft a message that appeals to emotion and uses stories. Talk from the heart and share the big picture. Touch on intrinsic motivators of mastery, autonomy and meaning. Celebrate successes.

All-hands are usually one of the only opportunities for many employees to talk directly with the founders and the C-level executives. Do not skip the Q&A part. If you make your all-hands a one-way broadcast, you will miss an opportunity. People want to feel heard. All-hands can build a culture of transparency. During the Q&A, you may also identify issues that would not surface otherwise. You could have town halls that are simply 'Ask Me Anything' sessions with the leaders. They can be effective in inspiring employees.

You need to be careful when handling questions. I know of a CEO who started having all-hands meetings, only to demotivate his company when he got defensive with the employees' questions and replied to them in a cynical, demeaning way. Have people submit questions and vote on the most pressing issues in advance, so that you can prepare for some of them. This also will allow for anonymity. We cannot overestimate the courage it takes to raise a question or a concern in front of the whole company.

The media company Hollis Co. puts special attention on how they run their weekly all-hands meetings.[8] They start with gratitude. The CEO selects five volunteers who share one small thing they are grateful for at the moment. Then they connect with their values by giving an award to the employee who has most embodied their values in the last week. The winner of the previous week's award describes the contribution of the person who has won this week, without revealing who they are. People try to guess. When the reveal happens, the crowd goes wild. These awards encourage employees to act on the company values daily, and to look for them in their colleagues' behaviour. For the closure of the meeting, they connect with the company's mission, which is to serve their community.

They have someone from their customer support department read an uplifting note by a member of their community or a customer.

All-hands meetings are a wonderful tool to shape culture and inspire people.

Summary

In order to connect with others in your meeting, you need to take care of yourself first. Your likeability and credibility are crucial to building relationships with clients and colleagues.

Table 6 summarizes the practices we have looked at in this chapter to promote your own well-being and enhance your connection with others.

| Table 6: How to Connect with Yourself and Others

Nurture and connect with yourself	Connect with others	Build authority
Take care of your body Take care of your mind	Empathy Authenticity Appreciation	Choose your words wisely Adopt a conversational speed Get to the point Own your space Project your voice

Use your one-to-ones to coach your direct reports and your all-hands to shape culture and inspire action.

Now that you have made sure that people will connect and listen to you in your meetings, let's see how you can make sure your participants will also be heard.

8   Ensure That People Speak Up in Your Meetings .

We meet because we want to tap into the collective knowledge and brainpower of groups. To achieve that, we need two key conditions in our meetings: inclusion and psychological safety. First, the participants need to feel welcome, socially accepted and valued in our meetings. That means they need to feel they have an equal chance to contribute and be listened to. Second, the participants need to feel that they can take an interpersonal risk in the meeting, share ideas, bring up problems, and disagree. Let's explore how we build an inclusive and safe environment in our meetings.

How to be inclusive in your meetings

We are programmed to quickly label people and decide who is in and who is out. We do it the moment we enter a bus and choose who to sit next to. We do it at the dinner party when everyone starts taking their seats, and we quickly start thinking about who we want to spend the next two hours with. We do it in meetings, deciding who to invite and who to listen to.

An inclusive meeting is a meeting where everyone has an equal opportunity to participate and be heard. That does not mean that everyone should participate equally in every meeting. Some people's opinion might be more relevant for the topic at hand. Neither does it mean we should strive for consensus or even majority rule. But we do want to make sure that we avoid people monopolizing the discussion and that everyone gets a chance to contribute if they want to. When MIT researchers studied the collective intelligence of groups, they found no correlation with the intelligence of the individuals in the group. But the collective intelligence, and therefore their ability to perform, was determined by how equally the members participated in the discussion, and by the proportion of women in the group.[1]

Most companies fail to have inclusive meetings. According to research, women tend to speak up less in meetings, and when they do, they are interrupted a lot more than men.[2] Also, they tend to get less credit for their ideas.[3] Whereas men with expertise tend to be *more* influential, women with expertise tend to be *less* so.[4] Displays of confidence and directness *decrease* women's influence but *increase* men's.[5] Phenomena like manterrupting, mansplaining and bropriating happen in the workplace every single day. We need to look out for them in our meetings.

LGBTQ+ minorities often do not feel included in meetings either. Some 53 per cent of LGBTQ+ employees have heard a joke about being gay or lesbian at work, many times in meetings. Also, one in five have had co-workers imply that they should dress in a more feminine or masculine way.[6] Sometimes these comments or microaggressions are well intentioned. Nonetheless, they may still affect how welcome an employee feels at our meeting. In addition, we need to bear in mind how easy we make it for people to share any information about their personal life at the beginning of our meetings. Research in both the US and the UK shows that almost half of LGBTQ+ employees are closeted at work. That means that when everyone speaks about their partner, children or what they did at the weekend, half of the LGBTQ+ employees in the meeting feel the need to hold back. Of course, this can be distracting and exhausting!

A study in the UK showed that BAME employees are more likely than those from a white British background to say they have experienced discrimination, and that they have felt the need to change aspects of their behaviour to 'fit' into the workplace.[7] Code-switching is when black people change their behaviour, speech or style in order to make the other people around them more comfortable, and to increase their possibilities of fair treatment. Many black people code-switch in their work meetings, and it comes with a great psychological cost.[8] How welcome do LGBTQ+ and BAME employees feel in your meetings?

Introverts are another group who tend to struggle in meetings where the people with the loudest voice monopolize the conversation. Ageism also plays a role – and it can go both ways, depending on the topic. For a social media strategy, we believe a 25-year-old's opinion is more valid than a 55-year-old's, but the tables are turned when we talk about a potential acquisition. The lion's share of the work for making a meeting feel inclusive lies with the leader. What leaders say and do makes a difference of up to 70 per cent as to whether an individual feels included.[9] How can you help make your meetings more inclusive? Here are some tips.

Find an easy way to signal when inclusion norms are broken

Inclusion norms are often broken in meetings by dismissive or sarcastic comments, inappropriate jokes, interruptions, and more. We need to find a way to raise awareness when this happens so that the group can learn and not repeat the same mistakes. Being aware of their own biases is one of the most important characteristics of a leader who is perceived as inclusive by their team.[10]

By ensuring that people speak up when they feel offended, you can create a more relaxed environment. No need to walk on eggshells. If a participant inadvertently says something insensitive, others will let them know straight away. There is a problem, though. It feels awkward to interrupt the flow of the meeting to let someone know that they have committed an inclusion faux pas. We need to make it easy, quick – and, ideally, somewhat fun.

For this purpose, I have used little red flags in some of my meetings. I place them on the table so that every participant can reach one. If someone feels an inclusion norm has been broken, they just raise the red flag. It is a lot easier to do that than state that you have been interrupted or ignored. It also brings a sense of humour and light-heartedness to something that is usually uncomfortable. Introduce this to the group and explain that, in order for all of you to become aware of your biases, you want people to raise the flags when they observe a non-inclusive behaviour. I know some other companies have used bells or a safe word to do the same thing. For virtual meetings, you may use the raise of the hand function or show a Post-it note of a certain colour.

Invite people to contribute

One of the best ways to make sure everyone has a chance to speak is the round robin. Participants take their turn to share their opinion on the issue at hand. While I dislike round robins where people give updates, a round robin where people give their opinion can be useful. To avoid needless repetition, you can allow people to simply say they agree with what was said previously.

Another way to invite participation is by asking questions. When thirty high-ranking women were asked to name the one thing they would change about how men treat them in meetings, 38 per cent said: 'Ask us direct questions'; or, 'Bring us into the discussion.'[11] Women are not the only ones. For example, in many Asian cultures, participants may expect someone to ask for their opinion before they offer it, unlike their western counterparts.

In virtual meetings, inclusion is even harder. Turn-taking is more difficult.[12] People who talk a lot in meetings talk even longer virtually as they do not see the non-verbal signs from the group that they need to wrap up. As a facilitator, you must make sure that everyone who wants to speak gets a chance. You can use the technology to launch a poll, do screen sharing, raise your hand, or submit questions and comments in the chatbox.

It is worth noting that when the meetings happen in person, but someone is dialling in remotely, it is a lot more difficult for them to participate. You need to be aware of that difficulty and potential exclusion, and try to mitigate it. The company Trello goes as far as to have everyone join the meeting from their laptops when even one participant is remote, to level the playing field.

Interrupt interruptions

Meeting leaders may want to interrupt people who like the sound of their own voice and monopolize the meeting. The clock is ticking, and you may get impatient when someone is going off at a tangent. The urge to interrupt is understandable, but you need to be aware of the harm interruptions do in a meeting. Use them sparingly, as they can be detrimental to inclusion, and be conscious of the trade-offs.

First, as we have already mentioned, interruptions are not distributed equally. Women and minorities tend to be interrupted a lot more than their colleagues. Second, if someone is interrupted and does not feel heard, they are a lot less likely to commit to the decisions of the group. Being interrupted can lead to a lot of frustration. Third, some people evolve their thinking while talking. Countless times in my coaching practice, I have seen people change their opinion or come up with a new brilliant idea while talking. There is something magical that happens in our thinking when someone is listening to us attentively.

So, even if you feel you are wasting time when you do not interrupt people, you might be saving time by helping people come up with better ideas and increasing the chances that participants will commit to the group's decisions. If you are pressed for time, give people an indication of how long their contribution should be. When you see someone interrupting another participant in the meeting, stop them and say something like: 'Wait a minute, John, I would like Sarah to finish her point first.'

I know that refraining from interrupting can be extremely hard when you have people who talk too much in your meeting. The other participants will be watching closely, to see how you deal with this issue. Treat the talkative person with respect, otherwise you will send the message that speaking up is unwelcome. But you also need to make sure they do not derail your whole meeting and drown out other voices.

After you have heard the talkative person, you can summarize what they said and then say: 'I would like now to hear from other people.' If they keep repeating their argument, summarize it and say: 'You have repeated this a few times. What point do you believe is not understood?' Sometimes it helps to give vocal people a note-taking role, as this will force them to listen to what other people say.

Repeat ideas from under-represented groups to amplify them

The women in the Obama administration had read the statistics about women getting less credit for their ideas, and being listened to less. Here is what they did.

> So female staffers adopted a meeting strategy they called 'amplification': When a woman made a key point, other women would repeat it, giving credit to its author. This forced the men in the room to recognize the contribution – and denied them the chance to claim the idea as their own.
> 'We just started doing it, and made a purpose of doing it. It was an everyday thing,' said one former Obama aide who requested anonymity to speak frankly. Obama noticed, she and others said, and began calling more often on women and junior aides.[13]

The 'amplification' strategy seems to have paid off: during Obama's second term, women gained parity with men in Obama's inner circle.

You can use the amplification strategy in your meeting with under-represented groups that you know are more likely to be ignored. What is important here is to amplify rather than appropriate, and the difference lies in giving credit to the originator of the idea. When you see someone repeating and appropriating someone else's point, step in and say something like: 'Yes, I liked Sarah's point, and I am glad you like it too.'

Use breakouts to make your meetings introvert-friendly

Meetings can be a difficult setting for many introverts. They need more time to process the data, and they also feel more comfortable in smaller groups. You have to cater to their needs if you are going to access their brilliant ideas. Have people discuss their opinions in pairs first. This will feel a lot safer to your introvert participants. Then ask each one of them to share the other's opinion with the group, or to share their freshest thinking after it has matured through the dialogue.

Doing breakouts has become a lot easier for many remote-meeting platforms. Other rooms may not be available during in-person meetings, or you may not want to waste time going to a different room and coming back. Breakouts in the same room can be noisy and distracting. Most of this friction dissipates with virtual breakouts. Many videoconferencing apps offer this capability with the click of a button.

I learned a technique from Professor David Clutterbuck that is great when your group is divided into two camps: the 'extroverts' wanting to take action, and the 'introverts' who have their doubts. Professor Clutterbuck suggests you send the 'extroverts' to another room (or virtual breakout) with a task to identify everything that could go wrong with their idea. In the meantime, the 'introverts' continue deliberating, as this is what they need – more time. When the two groups come back, they are closer together in their thinking. Consider allowing your participants time to process the data before or at the beginning of the meeting. If it is a Define or Develop meeting, you may want to let people know that it is OK for them to send you additional thoughts and ideas after the meeting.

How to foster psychological safety in your meetings

Inclusion means giving participants an equal opportunity to participate and be heard. However, it does not guarantee that when they do speak, they will voice the difficult stuff – the dissenting views, the mistakes and the vulnerabilities. For that to happen, you need psychological safety.

I had started managing a new account during my sales days, and I wanted to do a great job. In one of our meetings, the client expressed a complaint regarding another team in my company that was also working with them. I talked to the manager responsible and passed on the complaint. He invited me to come to their team's weekly meeting with his director and share what I had learned. 'Oh,' I thought, naively, 'these insights must be so useful, he wants everyone in the team to hear them from me.' I joined the team meeting and shared my client's complaint. Foolishly, I thought the team would appreciate this piece of intelligence as it allowed us to serve the customer better, but it turned out the manager had invited me because he did not feel safe to bring this complaint to the meeting himself.

The director of the team shouted at me and said: 'Your client is smoking weed!' I was shocked. Nobody wants to be yelled at, especially from a person of authority. For months after this initial encounter, I found myself losing my words when I was in front of that director.

Why did I become speechless when I was confronted with this director after that fateful meeting? My brain had associated a fight-flight-freeze response with being around him. A critical comment from a boss, a dismissive remark from a colleague, or a subordinate's provocation are often perceived as a life-or-death threat. We go into 'act first, think later' mode. We cannot think strategically or problem-solve. You can see how this dynamic could negatively impact the quality of your meetings – and, quite frankly, your business.

You may think this director was a bully. That you are nothing like that. The problem is that most of us are not aware of how scary we are. And while we might be lovely and approachable most of the time, having a bad day and showing a bit more impatience in a meeting is enough for people to think that it is not safe to speak up around us.

A year after launching my business and completing my MSc in coaching, I joined a team coaching training event at Oxford University. My business was growing rapidly, and I oozed confidence. To my disappointment, I realized that the class was for beginners. I felt impatient with people asking questions all the time. At the end of the training, a lady from my working group shared the feedback that she had been so intimidated by me that she had stopped contributing to the group. This time, I was the one scaring others. I would have never known, if it weren't for the structured feedback exercise the course required.

Fear to speak up can lead to disasters. Take a look at Nokia; it used to be the world leader in mobile phones. The company's market value declined by about 90 per cent in just six years, from 2007 to 2013, losing around US$100 billion. INSEAD

Professor Quy Huy did more than seventy interviews with Nokia employees to find out what happened.[14] His conclusion? It was fear that killed Nokia, even more than the iPhone. Senior leaders were described as temperamental, often shouting 'at the top of their lungs'. Middle managers were directly lying to their bosses during meetings, presenting the situation as more positive than it was. They masked the deficiencies of the Symbian product. Employees created a falsely positive bubble, to avoid the anger of their superiors, eventually leading the company to its downfall.

Another example is General Motors and the faulty-switch scandal. When GM launched vehicles with a switch-safety issue, at least 54 crashes occurred, and up to 100 people died. In 2014, GM recalled more than 20 million vehicles. Following an internal investigation, General Motors CEO Mary Barra publicly stated that the company's corporate culture had helped suppress the voices of employees who were alarmed about safety issues. 'Speaking up at meetings was not safe.'[15] In this case, the lack of psychological safety proved costly to human life.

I first learned about the concept of psychological safety while I was working at Google. Their people analytics department wanted to figure out what makes a great team. They studied 180 successful and unsuccessful teams over several years. Initially, they could not crack the code. They could not put their finger on what was the common thread across successful teams. Tenure, seniority, extraversion or individual performance did not matter. Consensus decision making, workload, or being located at the same office did not matter either.

It was only when they stumbled on Professor Amy Edmondson's research on psychological safety that they figured it out. Psychological safety was the most important attribute that separated effective teams from the ineffective. It made by far the biggest difference in team performance compared to any other attribute they studied.

What does this mean for your meetings? You can have the perfect agenda and a very competent team, but unless there is psychological safety in the group, your meetings will not be successful. It is that important.

So, what is psychological safety? Edmondson defined psychological safety as the ability to take an interpersonal risk in a team. This means that the team members can bring up ideas or issues without being afraid of the consequences.

Do you remember a meeting where you held back and did not share an issue or an idea? Most of us can. People do not speak up because they are afraid of two things: that others are going to see them in a negative light, or that they are going to harm their relationships with others. People stay silent because they are playing not to lose rather than playing to win. So, how can you make your meetings more psychologically safe?

Verbally reward people when they speak up

This is the most important strategy, as people learn to do more of what brings them reward and less of what brings them pain. Make the meeting's participants feel that their contributions are welcome by nodding and sharing statements that show you understand: 'I see what you are saying', 'I understand.' Repeat or summarize their points, as this sends the signal that you have heard them. A leader who seems distracted, maybe on her phone or laptop, does not invite team members to speak up. They may feel that the leader does not have the time or the patience to listen to them.

Welcome ideas, even if you do not agree with them. Welcome concerns, even if this slows down the decision making. Reward an employee who calls out a mistake. Celebrate learning. Ray Dalio, founder of the Bridgewater fund, goes so far as to say that holding back ideas is unethical behaviour.

Model honesty and vulnerability

One of the best ways to send a signal that it is OK to be honest is for the leader to model that behaviour. You can share a personal story at the beginning of the meeting. You can talk about your mistakes. Pixar executives, for example, share the errors the company has made in the onboarding of every new employee. This helps them get across the message that even though they are successful, they make a lot of mistakes, and everyone is encouraged to challenge their superiors.

Create a structure for speaking up

It is hard to foster psychological safety when your meeting design is composed of a series of PowerPoint presentations. Ensure there is time in your meeting agenda for discussion, ideation, bringing up issues, and asking questions. You will make it a lot easier for people to speak up.

When you lead a group that is not yet psychologically safe, look into ways to invite anonymous participation. I learned another great exercise from Professor David Clutterbuck. Have the group write on Post-it notes a sensitive topic that the group avoids discussing. The proverbial elephant in the room. Collect all the Post-its and put them in a box. Make it clear to people that it is safe to discuss difficult issues, and there will be no negative repercussions. Then have people take a Post-it out and argue its point as passionately as if it was their own. By not knowing who wrote that point, the group can feel safer to discuss it. You can adapt this exercise for a virtual meeting by submitting the sensitive topics to an anonymous survey.

Anonymous complaints or idea boxes are other ways to help the group speak up. Allow a lot of time, as you do not want to open up sensitive issues without giving people time to process them. The more uncomfortable conversations you have in your meetings, the easier and safer it gets.

Measure your current psychological safety

As a leader, you are likely to overestimate the psychological safety you have in your meetings and team. It is important to measure it. Try the following exercise in one of your meetings.

> **Step 1:** Write the definition of psychological safety – 'the ability to take an interpersonal risk in a team' – on a flipchart or a slide, and give some examples to bring it to life.
> - I am able to bring up problems and tough issues in the meeting
> - People in this meeting do not reject others for being different
> - If I say something wrong in this meeting, it will not be held against me
> - My contributions to the meeting are valued
>
> **Step 2:** Ask your team to anonymously write on a Post-it note or in an online survey how psychologically safe they feel in the team, on a score from 1 to 10.
>
> **Step 3:** Share the average score with the team.
>
> **Step 4:** Go around the table and ask everyone to share one experience they had in this meeting that helped them feel psychologically safe and one that achieved the opposite. This

helps raise awareness of what behaviours undermine psychological safety and what behaviours encourage it. The last time I did this exercise with a team, they raised their psychological safety score from 7.5 to 8.3 within six months.

Psychological safety is what sets high-performing teams and successful meetings apart. Putting in the effort to measure it – and create it – is well worth it.

How Pixar fosters psychological safety

Pixar is one company that produced nothing but hits in the thirty years after its founding, in 1986. Pixar's co-founder Ed Catmull attributed the company's success to its culture of psychological safety, which helps its employees generate innovative ideas, take risks, and also maintain an incredibly high standard of work. There are a few key cornerstone meetings that help keep this culture alive and bring about those results.

The dailies meeting
Every day the Pixar animators show their unfinished work to their colleagues. This is uncomfortable. None of us likes to show unfinished work. But there are a lot of benefits. You can get ideas or criticism early, without investing days going in the wrong direction. You can inspire your colleagues with your work. There are no surprises. Everyone is encouraged to send feedback by email to the animators, explaining what they liked, what they did not like, and why. The dailies happen every day at 9 a.m. in a small movie theatre that seats about fifty people, and they last for about an hour. During that hour they get through between fifteen and twenty movie shots,

and provide notes and feedback. All animators can contribute, while the director holds the final say. The dailies is a Do meeting, as it focuses on the implementation. How can you adopt this type of feedback in your company? Showing visual work – like presentations, designs or ads – is one obvious way. But how about listening to a sales call, watching a presentation, or reading emails to clients to provide feedback on improving them? Uncomfortable? Yes. But also transformational.

The braintrust meeting

This is a meeting with the eight directors and the Pixar CEO. When a director and a producer think they need help, they convene the group and show the current version of their work in progress. Then they have a two-hour discussion about making the movie better. Ed Catmull explains: 'There's no ego. Nobody pulls any punches to be polite. This works because all the participants have come to trust and respect one another. They know it's far better to learn about problems from colleagues when there's still time to fix them than from the audience after it's too late.'[16] What also makes this meeting work is that it is up to the director to use the feedback, or not. The braintrust is mostly a Define meeting, as the objective is to identify the right problems to solve.

The braintrust has a purely consultative role and no authority. This is key. It allows the group to speak freely, even if their ideas are not fully developed. It frees people to ask for help, as they know that they will still have the final say.

Post-mortems

At Pixar, they realized something I have seen again and again in my coaching work. Even though people learn a lot from doing post-mortems, they don't like doing them. Post-mortems, or retrospectives, are meetings to review what you did in a certain project, and what you can learn from it. When you finish a project, you want to congratulate everyone rather than see what went wrong. You also want to move on to the next thing. Pixar learned from a lot of failed post-mortems, and they have tweaked them to increase their impact. First, they ask the group to list the top five things they would do again, and the top five things they wouldn't do. This makes it easier, as you balance the positive and the negative, and you are forward-looking instead of merely regurgitating what already happened.

Also, they have a look at the data to make the post-mortem more objective and neutral. You will be surprised to see how much quantitative data you can find regarding a project. How much time did it take compared to the original planning? How often did something need to be reworked? How complete was the work before it got passed over to another department? Post-mortems are Define meetings: you create a shared view of reality and you agree on goals and problems to be solved in future projects.

Pixar's meetings are the key element of their safe and creative culture. They are designed in a way that encourages people to speak up.

Summary

Inclusion and psychological safety are the foundations for a successful meeting. In Table 7, you can see the best practices shared in this chapter to create those fruitful conditions in your meetings.

| Table 7: Inclusion and Psychological Safety

Inclusion	Psychological safety
Signal when inclusion norms are broken	Verbally reward people for speaking up
Invite people to contribute	Model honesty and vulnerability
Interrupt interruptions	
Amplify opinions from groups that tend to be ignored	Create a structure for speaking up
Use breakouts to make your meetings introvert-friendly	Measure your current psychological safety

Unleashing the potential of the People in your meeting requires self-care, connection, inclusion and psychological safety. Next, we will move on to review some of our meeting Processes, starting with how we can reduce the time wasted in our meetings.

9 Reduce the Time Wasted in Meetings

If you find yourself trapped in back-to-back meetings that drain your energy, this chapter is for you. In the first part of the book, we saw how you can achieve your meeting's Purpose by following the 4D Framework. In the previous two chapters, we talked about creating the conditions for the People attending your meetings to bring their best, including yourself. In the next four chapters, we will have a look at some key meetings Processes, and we will start by reducing the unproductive time you spend in your meetings. There is a way out, believe me.

While we all dislike wasteful, unnecessary meetings, we constantly find ourselves in them. In this chapter, we will explore some of the reasons why this is happening – and what you can do about it. Together, we will do a spring-cleaning of your organization's calendar so that you have only meetings that spark joy. Meetings that bring people together to achieve 4D outcomes on important topics. Using the tips in this chapter, many of my clients have reduced the time they spend in meetings by more than half. Imagine what you could do with all this extra time! For your work, and for yourself.

Put a monetary value on the problem

How much does the time wasted in unnecessary, irrelevant or badly run meetings cost your organization? You cannot manage what you cannot measure. Here is how to put a monetary value on the problem.

> **Step 1:** List the recurring meetings your team has. How many hours per week do they spend in recurring meetings?
>
> **Step 2:** Launch a simple survey of the participants. Ask them what percentage of the time they spend in these meetings is useful and what percentage is wasted.
>
> **Step 3:** Use a meeting cost calculator (you can find one online) to turn the time wasted into money.

This will help you to quantify the problem and also to pitch any changes in your meetings to your stakeholders. Let's say you have a team of ten people and they waste two hours a week in bad or irrelevant meetings, and their average yearly salary is $80,000. In that case you are squandering around $52,000 a year, according to the HBR (*Harvard Business Review*) meeting cost calculator. Would you be happy if you could save the company $52K a year? What if you could do that across your organization? We could now start talking about millions. And when we talk about millions, the C-suite starts to listen.

Protect no-meetings blocks of time and cluster your meetings

I have no meetings on two working days of my week. Creating that meeting-free zone has had the most significant effect on my productivity and well-being. The days that I have coaching sessions and meetings, I focus on being present. The days that I don't, I can do writing, learning and strategy without interruptions.

You will need to establish a no-meetings day throughout the company if you want this strategy to work. It is very hard for individual employees to do this on their own without the company's support. Establish a day a week, or even a morning a week to start with, when all employees are meeting-free. This is the time for deep work, creative or strategic thinking. You may want to avoid having all your regular team and departmental meetings on Monday morning. This is the time when your people are at their best, recharged from the weekend. Let them do some deep, individual work on their core function, and schedule your meetings later in the day or the week. The optimal time to book a team meeting is Tuesday at 2.30 p.m., according to a study conducted by YouCanBookMe scheduling firm.[1] They analysed data from more than two million responses to 530,000 meeting invitations.

Many of my clients have implemented 'office hours' with great success. They will block a couple of hours every week, and employees can book fifteen- or thirty-minute slots to discuss whatever they want. This helps the leader check the pulse of the organization and be accessible, while avoiding interspersed meetings throughout the day or week. In general, try to cluster meetings in blocks of time, rather than offer your whole calendar for anyone to book. Aim to leave half-hour gaps between one meeting and another, to be able to successfully context-switch.

Avoid holding meetings out of habit

Most people in business are familiar with zero-based budgeting. Every year, you create your budget from scratch, without taking for granted that you will continue to incur the same expenses you did the previous year. You can do the same with one of the most precious resources of your organization – time.

Cancel all recurring meetings for a defined period of time

Many teams are searching for items to discuss in their meeting, instead of having a meeting because there is something to discuss. Managers at Dropbox wanted to put a stop to needless meetings, and they went all in. One day they sent an email to all employees with the subject line: 'Armeetingeddon has landed.' They cancelled all recurring meetings for two weeks. After the hiatus, employees had to agree on which meetings needed to come back. In the two years after Armeetingeddon, Dropbox tripled the number of employees at its headquarters, but their meetings were shorter and more productive.[2]

Avoid meeting creep

Assume your recurring meeting is not happening unless someone confirms the meeting and justifies its purpose. When someone needs to put themselves on the line for a meeting to happen, the likelihood of the meeting being useful increases.

When you add a new recurring meeting, consider whether you need to end another existing meeting.

Make meetings optional

Eric Lindblad, vice-president of Boeing's 737 programme, knew that meetings were an expensive way to communicate. So, he made them voluntary. What's more, he made it OK for people to leave a meeting before it was finished if they thought their time was better used elsewhere. If the participants cannot leave or skip the meeting physically, they will do so mentally. They will check out, do other work on their laptop or phone, or browse on social media. Eric used his meetings attendance as a feedback mechanism. If people did not attend, he would look into improving the value they were getting out of his meetings.

One of the highest attendances I have seen is in the voluntary, regular ninety-minute innovation meeting run at the agency VMLY&R Asia. Even if the meeting is optional, everyone wants to join it, as it is well run. The group's leader and chief innovation officer, Keith Timimi, uses design thinking approaches to stimulate the participants' creativity and solve business problems. Participants not only attend but they consider this meeting the best part of their week.

Making meetings optional will not work as well as eliminating unnecessary meetings altogether. This is because most of us have a fear of being cut out of the action. Even if the meeting is optional, we are likely to attend in the hope that the meeting might be useful and help us connect with our colleagues.

Create knowledge assets

One of my clients was the most experienced person in his team. He knew important information about the history of the product and as a result he was invited to many meetings to contribute his knowledge. He was exhausted! He fixed this problem by working with HR to create a proper onboarding process for new members of the team, as well as good documentation and FAQs, so that people did not have to go to him any more. I get requests every week to jump on a call to give advice to an aspiring new coach. I now point most of them to the articles I have written on the topic. These assets save me tons of time and are a lot more comprehensive and helpful for the people who reach out.

If you find yourself being invited to meetings to say the same things, consider creating an asset that will answer the most common questions. It requires an upfront investment of time and effort, but it will save you a lot of time in the future.

Decline wasteful meetings

It is no surprise that billionaires understand their most precious resource is time, and they get comfortable with saying no to meetings. Warren Buffett famously said that the difference between successful and very successful people is that the latter say no to almost everything. Billionaire entrepreneur Mark Cuban agrees and argues: 'Only attend a meeting if someone writes you a check.'[3]

For some time, I tried to follow Mark Cuban's advice. I would only accept meetings from clients or prospective clients. Soon, though, I found myself wanting to have more meetings, to connect with my partners and team. I realized that what is important is not necessarily having meetings only when someone writes you a cheque, but knowing why you are having your meetings, and being OK to say no when the meeting does not fit with your goals.

Many of us attend unnecessary meetings to prove our usefulness to the organization. We know our managers have availability and recency bias, just like everyone else. They keep at the front of their minds the people they see often and recently. Just like a product needs to have several communication touchpoints before we trust it and consider buying it, we also clock our touchpoints for our next promotion by attending many meetings, useful or not.

In most organizations, you will need to work with your manager on reducing the number of meetings you attend. Persuade them that your time will be more effectively spent in more value-creating activities than some of your current meetings. For the meetings you do attend, go for quality over quantity and show up present, energized and ready to make a difference.

Here are some ways you can reject attending a meeting without harming your professional relationships.

- 'I am not the best person to attend this meeting. [*Enter other person's name*] will have more relevant input.'
- 'I am working on another project at the moment. Could you please brief me about the outcome of the meeting afterwards, or include me in the follow-up email?'
- 'What type of input do you need from me? Could I give it to you before the meeting?'
- 'I see that the meeting has no agenda or clear objective. Is this meeting needed?'

- 'I see that only a small part of the meeting is relevant to me. Can I join for only that part of the meeting?'

By saying no to meetings that are not the best use of your time, you say yes to other more important work, you protect your energy reserves, and you can make more of a difference where it matters.

Stop holding meetings for the wrong reasons

We have unproductive, frustrating meetings because many of them are not scheduled to achieve a 4D outcome. What's more, we still hold them because we believe meetings are the necessary price to pay for a participative culture and collaboration. This belief is even more entrenched for remote teams. Meetings build an inclusive, participatory culture when they are used to Define Problems, Develop Ideas, Decide and get stuff Done. They achieve the opposite when they are scheduled for the wrong reasons.

Let's take a look at some not-so-good reasons to schedule a meeting, and what you can do instead.

Information transfer and status updates

Most companies simply have meetings to update each other. Let's put a stop to that. There are better ways to transfer information and give updates. I know this idea is controversial. If you do not believe me that status meetings need to disappear, let's look at the data.

According to a survey by Clarizen, almost half of employed Americans would prefer another unpleasant activity to attending status meetings. The unpleasant activities listed included getting a mullet hairstyle (7 per cent), watch paint dry (17 per cent), and even undergo root canal treatment (8 per cent).[4] If that's not a cry for help to stop status meetings, I don't know what is.

So, how do you keep the information flowing without meetings? Most information sharing does not need to be synchronous, and most updates do not need to interrupt someone's work to be successful. Email, documents, blogs, intranet posts or messaging are the obvious solutions.

Some people get even more creative. When I worked at Google, Kirk Perry was the president of our global clients and agencies department. In his first year as a leader, he got feedback that his employees wanted to hear more from him. The obvious answer would be to start doing more all-hands meetings. But all-hands are expensive, and the information did not need to be delivered in real time. Kirk had a different idea. He started doing selfie videos on his phone with updates, and he emailed the link to us. I loved those videos. I still remember a video Kirk shot following an important meeting with our largest client. I found it fascinating to hear his thoughts about our business, first-hand, after such a crucial meeting. I could watch these videos when I had the time, without disrupting my workday.

You can upload your video or audio updates as private files on a hosting platform. Not only will you be able to see the number of views but you will also know the exact second people get bored and drop off. You can learn and make the next one better.

The whole world of advertising has moved from the interruption of TV ads to the consent-driven content marketing of video and social media. Our business communications, though, have hardly evolved. We should be moving from mandatory, all-hands meetings to interesting, targeted content that people choose to consume.

LEADx, a leadership development company, was built to be remote first. Every day, all employees get an automated message at 4.45 p.m. with the question: 'What did you COMPLETE today?'[5] They spend fifteen seconds responding, and it magically sends the updates to everyone. They all stay in the loop, and are motivated by each other's progress. Basecamp is another company that uses automated software to replace their daily and weekly stand-up status meetings.

It is best to spend your meeting time on solving issues, generating ideas and making decisions rather than giving updates. If you decide to do status updates in your operational meetings, at least have a rule that people need to stick to a certain time slot, usually a minute. There is only one type of update that is best done live: an update that can create an intense emotional reaction. These updates can be positive or negative.

I am sure you still remember the phone call that let you know you'd got a job, or a meeting where you learned about your promotion. Announce great news to your company live, to maximize the positive impact. Just as you would prefer to watch a concert or a live game, the same goes with the big, emotional updates in business.

Similarly, if you have bad news to share, it is better to do it in person. This could be feedback, budget cuts, redundancies, or any other update that may cause negative emotions. Just as you would not break up with someone in a text message, don't deliver emotional news to your colleagues and employees via email.

Convenience for the leader
One of the reasons leaders schedule unnecessary meetings is because it saves them time and effort. Imagine you have some updates to share with your team. If you were to write an email,

it would take you an hour. You can call a half-hour meeting with your eight direct reports and share the update and finish sooner. With the meeting, you save half an hour, and it feels great, you can go back to work. However, you have absorbed eight half-hours from other people. The organization as a whole has invested 4.5 hours for this update to happen. As much as a leader's time costs more, it rarely costs that many times more than their direct reports' time.

Leaders also use meetings to find out what is going on in the business, without having to do one-to-one meetings or read memos. Again, a convenience for the leader, but it results in a lot of time wasted in meetings. The meeting becomes a series of parallel discussions, with the rest of the participants waiting their turn and feeling bored or frustrated. A project-management tool that everyone keeps updated would inform the leader at a glance whether everything is on track, without the need for more meetings.

A few companies, such as Seagate and Boeing, are experimenting with giving their managers feedback on the 'load' they are putting on the organization in terms of meetings, emails and instant messages.[6] Research has shown that for every manager you add to the organization, you create the equivalent of 1.5 people's workload, and up to 3 people's workload for executives. This is their own workload plus the workload they create for others. As part of a programme in Seagate, managers received a report sharing data on their organizational load and comparing it to other managers at their level. They became more conscious about putting burdens on other people's time. Is there a way you can provide feedback to your leaders on their organizational load? Or, more drastically, is there a way to simplify your organizational structure, starting at the top? Your number of meetings will go down.

I was discussing with one VP whether he would be open to making his weekly team meeting optional. He immediately frowned with defensiveness and anger. He said: 'No way. It is *my* meeting. Period.' He quickly changed the topic, making it clear that I should not continue this conversation. I reflected on this incident. What was it about making his meeting optional that was so threatening for this leader?

Often, a manager gets to really feel like a leader of a whole team only during their team meeting. Otherwise, they are just a manager of individual direct reports. Meetings satisfy deep psychological needs for the leader, including a need for confirmation of their authority. This is a human need, and one that is more likely to be fulfilled by fewer, more successful meetings.

Networking

One leader of a geographically dispersed team told me that his team complained about the quality of their monthly meeting. I observed the meeting, which was a round robin of status updates from the disengaged participants. I gave them the feedback that their meeting fell flat because they were not achieving any of the 4D outcomes.

The leader shared that they were not really a team. They managed different clients, and the only thing they had in common was reporting to the same manager. The objective of their monthly meeting was for them to connect, as it was the only opportunity they had to do so. The problem was that the team was not aware that this was the objective – and hearing a series of status updates that were not relevant to their own work was the worst way for them to build meaningful relationships and team spirit. They all dreaded that meeting.

We came up with a makeover of their monthly meeting. Since the objective was to connect, they renamed it 'Monthly

Tea' and had a social gathering where they could informally catch up. The team members also agreed that they could call a Develop meeting at any time. In that Develop meeting they could ask the group for ideas on a challenge they were facing, similar to Pixar's braintrust. This would provide a way to productively help each other and to leverage the group's experience and knowledge. A few months later, that group felt more cohesive than ever.

Workplace cohesion, the interpersonal connection among employees, is crucial. Ben Waber from Humanyze, a people analytics company, found that cohesion was far and away the single most important factor with regard to productivity and stress for the employees he studied.[7] This point is difficult to overstate. To get a sense of the magnitude of the importance of cohesion in worker productivity, Waber found cohesion was about thirty times more important than experience.

Google's research found psychological safety to be by far the most important factor for performance, while Humanyze found group cohesion to outperform all other variables. These results do not necessarily contradict each other. They both point to the fact that investing in the relationships that exist in the group, building trust and openness and a sense of belonging, irrespective of what you say, are by far the highest ROI (return on investment) development activities you can do.

How do you create this precious cohesion? Well, Waber is emphatic that meetings don't create the kind of cohesion essential to great teams. His findings showed that what matters is the social time people spend together, such as when their lunch breaks overlap.

Dr Sandy Pentland from MIT argues: 'Social time turns out to be deeply critical to team performance, often accounting for more than 50 per cent of positive changes in communication patterns.'[8] If you have meetings with the sole objective of building connectedness, you may be better off replacing them with social time. Here are some ideas of what you can do.

Have a weekly event where people can have some food and unwind together

At Google we had TGIF, at Twitter they have Tea Thursdays. Choose something that works for your culture, and have the social time in a different space from where you usually work. If your team is remote, you can have those social gatherings virtually. Admittedly, it is a lot harder to psychologically separate meetings and social gatherings in a virtual environment. You are in the same work space and you use the same tools: your laptop and your videoconferencing app. When I host virtual social time for teams, I provide more structure to the conversation than I would in an in-person social event. I select a series of interesting questions, such as 'What would you do if you won the lottery?' or 'What was the best moment you had with friends?' and send the group to discuss them in virtual breakouts. You may ask the participants to have a special dress code for social gatherings, so that they differentiate them from the day-to-day work. Informal discussions build the intimacy and trust of the group. You may want to make those events optional, as they do not work for everyone, especially not for introverts.

Use social channels in your messaging services, where people can post things irrelevant to work and build a community – a parents' channel or a cooking channel, for example.

Encourage people to have social one-to-ones

If your employees work in a shared office, encourage them to have lunch together rather than at their desks. At Google, we had an internal tool that you could sign up to, and it would randomly pair you with a colleague for lunch. If you work remotely, a walk-and-talk phone call is a great way to get those steps in while getting to know a colleague. These one-to-one social interactions are more comfortable for introverts, who may find the company-wide social events painful.

Create shared experiences

This is challenging with a remote team. Giorgos Vareloglou, co-founder of digital consultancy Reborrn, faced a real challenge when the Covid-19 lockdown of March 2020 happened. A big part of his business was running design sprints around Europe. Vareloglou and his team quickly pivoted to a virtual format. They did not know how to replace the dinners and social time in the virtual environment. They got creative. The first question they asked themselves was how to replace the lunch-break experience, where people get together to enjoy lunch. They brought in chefs to run a super-fast cooking class with materials almost anyone would have in their fridge. Then they shared a lunch together. The result was great as it was, first and foremost, a lot of fun. People got to discuss each other's culinary skills and laugh about it. Cooking the same plate and sharing the same lunch with people around the globe gave them a strong sense of connection.

Next, Vareloglou and his team looked for a way to get the participants centred at the beginning of the day. They started it with some mindfulness, doing a fifteen-minute meditation with an expert. Finally, they wanted to create a shared experience that would allow the participants to let off some steam and have fun together. They organized a forty-minute improv theatre session with an expert where all the virtual participants could participate. The feedback they received was stellar. What shared experiences could you create for your group, especially when it is remote?

When organizing social activities, think about being as inclusive as possible. Try to schedule your social activities during working hours, but ideally at the start or end of the working day so that you do not break the flow of work. If social bonding happens after hours in the pub, this can leave parents at a disadvantage. Be aware that if all the social activities include alcohol, this might exclude the non-drinkers. Or if it is about sport, maybe not everyone can participate. One senior executive told me that he realized he had a lot of his casual business conversations in the changing rooms at the company's gym. This excluded women, obviously. When he noticed that, he made a conscious effort to create casual conversation opportunities outside this space.

Designing inclusive social experiences can be a challenge, as people have different preferences. Ask your team members to suggest and vote. Mix things up to satisfy different groups. Or default to some safe options (tea party, anyone?) that most people can enjoy.

Use the 4D Framework to coach your team

Work as a team to Define the goal on team cohesion and what the key challenges are. The exercises on feedback and identifying a team's toxic behaviours that I shared in previous chapters may be helpful here. Or run a Develop meeting to come up with ideas of how the team can build more trust. When the objective is to build togetherness and cohesion, old-style meetings won't cut it. You need to be clear about the desired outcome and prepare the session accordingly.

Connection is so important for successful meetings that you should always spend some time at the beginning to establish it (as we will see in Chapter 12). Then you can move on success-fully to Define, Develop, Decide or Do. While meetings need connection to be successful, connection does not necessarily need meetings – and it definitely does not need the typical status-update meetings. Social gatherings, common experiences, personal sharing in your written channels and team coaching sessions can work a lot better for that purpose.

Sharing best practices

Best practices are working methods that are superior to others. Every company tries to recognize the best practices and share them, so that people learn from each other and do not have to reinvent the wheel. This is especially important for big, multi-national companies where they might have many teams doing the same work. The problem is that we often share best practices with the wrong people at the wrong time. No one wants to waste time listening to an irrelevant presentation that has no value for them.

There is a simple fix for inefficient best-practice-sharing meetings. You need to create a process to match the supply and demand of best practices. Ask people to answer two questions:

- What are the best practices they can share with their colleagues?
- What are the best practices they need?

Then you can help do the matchmaking, delivering relevant content to the right audience at the time they need it. This may include meetings, but they will be smaller, shorter, focused and useful.

Internal social networks can work for this purpose as well. I am a member of a couple of entrepreneur groups on social media, and they have been invaluable. Whenever I have a question about how to do something, I post a question in my group, and I have great answers from people who have been-there-done-that, right when I need them.

You could bring this camaraderie to your internal corporate social networks. I have seen internal 'miscellaneous' email groups work well for that purpose. Encourage people to post their wins and questions. That way, best practice is delivered at the exact moment someone needs it the most. If you think people may not want to appear vulnerable by admitting they need help in a group that includes everyone, you can set up a group without the managers.

Collaboration

Leaders assume that the more meetings people have, the more they collaborate. This is not necessarily true. Research has shown that while the number of meetings has risen steadily since 2008, the amount of collaboration hasn't: 80 per cent of meetings happen within organizational silos and not across them.[9] You do not need to set up more meetings with the objective of collaboration. You will have collaboration by default if you hold successful 4D meetings.

Collaboration does not always need to be synchronous. A writer and an editor can collaborate closely and efficiently, but they may never meet. There are two advances in technology that have made collaboration easier without the need for meetings.

Project-management tools

There are plenty of these on the market. You can assign tasks to people, make updates, leave comments for each other, and know at a glance where everyone is with regard to the milestone they need to achieve.

Online documents

Little frustrates me more than when I collaborate with companies who do not use cloud-based documents. They have one poor person compiling different versions in a single document, rather than everyone working with one cloud version of the document simultaneously. Cloud documents allow everyone to insert their input on the same document while it is automatically updated and saved.

When you need input on a document, whether it is your sales presentation or your business plan, share it with your colleagues. They can read it in their own time, reflect on it, and share comments on the exact slide or line that they are referring to. They can also fill in their part without disrupting others. This is a more pleasant and effective process than requesting feedback on a document you present to people while asking them to process everything and think on their feet.

Summary

If we eliminate the wasteful meetings, our 4D meetings will be more successful. As people will have only purposeful meetings, their expectations will be higher. When their expectations are higher, they will come to the meeting better prepared and engaged. People will also be more engaged because they will treat their meeting time as precious, as they are not burdened by unnecessary meetings. In this chapter, we saw how you can eliminate wasteful meetings. You need to put numbers to the problem and cluster meetings together, protecting blocks of deep work. Avoid holding meetings out of habit, and practise ways to decline meetings that are a waste of your time.

A meeting is not always the best medium for achieving your goal. Table 8 summarizes the good and not-so-good reasons to have a meeting.

If your meeting goal relates to a 4D outcome on an important topic, a meeting is probably a good idea. If you want to run a meeting for another reason, think again. In this chapter, we have reviewed what you can do instead. Now that you have kept only useful 4D meetings in your calendar, we can go into more detail on how to prepare for them.

| Table 8: Reasons to Have a Meeting

More likely to need a meeting: 4D outcomes	Less likely to need a meeting
Define a shared view of reality, a goal or a problem	Information transfer and status updates
Develop ideas	Convenience for the leader
Decide on an important issue	Networking
Do! Execute, plan and inspire for action	Sharing best practices
	Collaboration

10 Prepare for a Successful Meeting

Top business thinker Peter Drucker said: 'Only three things happen naturally in organizations: friction, confusion, and underperformance. Everything else requires leadership.'[1]

If we do not want our meetings to be chaotic and ineffective, we need to prepare for them. Jared Spool, who has researched how design teams collaborate, observed: 'The more effective teams spent more time preparing for the meeting than the less effective teams. In setting up the meeting, they'd discuss the approach they'd use and exactly what they wanted to get out.'[2]

There are two essential elements of preparation for a successful meeting: agenda and attendee list.

How to form a successful agenda

When the meeting has an agenda, participants perceive it as more effective.[3] Participants can prepare their input to the topics. It is easier to stay focused on the issue at hand. You can save time by having people join only the parts relevant to them.

In one of the teams I coached, the team leader wrote down the topics he wanted to discuss, but did not share them with the team in advance or at any point in the meeting. As a result, the team would spend too much time deliberating the first issue, as they had no idea how many items were on the agenda. Crafting and sharing an agenda was an easy way to improve the quality of their meetings. So, here are some strategies to create a compelling agenda.

Separate strategic from operational meetings

People tend to spend a lot more time on trivial issues in their meetings than they spend on important ones. Research reveals that as much as 80 per cent of top management's time is devoted to issues that account for less than 20 per cent of a company's long-term value.[4] This phenomenon is called 'Parkinson's Law of Triviality' or the 'bicycle-shed effect'.

In his book *Parkinson's Law*, C. Northcote Parkinson talked about a committee that needed to approve the plans of a nuclear power plant and the plans for the bicycle shed next to the factory. The committee spent two minutes discussing the power plant and forty-five minutes debating the bicycle shed. People felt they had more expertise to offer regarding the bicycle shed.

We have seen it all too often. A company's leadership team spends more time deciding their Christmas card than their whole strategy in Asia. Or a sales team debates the colours of their presentation for hours, rather than discussing the content. When you have separate strategic and operational meetings, you can defer more day-to-day items to the operational meeting and focus your strategic meeting on the important issues. The company Intel uses that strategy and has mission meetings and process meetings.[5] Making that separation will minimize the time spent on items that represent very little value for your company.

But be aware that trivial issues will slip in – even in your most strategic meetings – as they can be a defence mechanism against the anxiety of the group. Just as we feel a temptation to check our social media when we are working on a complex, difficult task, groups will tend to be distracted when they feel stressed in the meeting, want to avoid making a difficult decision, or have uncomfortable conflict. As a meeting leader, be on the lookout for such avoidance mechanisms, and help the group work through them. Say something like: 'We are tending to get distracted from the topic at hand, and I wonder whether that is because we are finding the decision too stressful?' By holding up the mirror and starting an enquiry you can help the team get through the issues. If you perceive the stress going up in your meeting, you may also want to provide more structure to the discussion, which will add a sense of safety for the participants.

State the purpose of the meeting
It is important to be clear whether this is a Define, Develop, Decide or Do meeting. What is the outcome you are aiming for? How will you know if the meeting is successful? Communicate this on your agenda.

Seek input to the agenda
The participants will be more engaged in the meeting if they have a say in the agenda. Ask for input in advance of the meeting. You can use interviews, surveys or email, depending on how important the meeting is. At the very least, at the beginning of the meeting ask people to review and add items to the agenda if they need to.

Choose topics that require everyone's participation
Many teams use their meetings to have parallel conversations with the leader. This is a sure way to have the rest of the people

switch off and start typing on their laptops, as they feel their time is better spent elsewhere. Select topics that impact the entire team, or topics that the whole team can participate in. If you need to have individual conversations, hold them in a one-to-one setting.

Put the most important topics first

Content at the start of an agenda receives disproportionate amounts of time and attention, regardless of its importance.[6] The implication is clear: deal with your most important issues at the start of the meeting. Professor David Clutterbuck asks the participants to rate the urgency of the agenda items from 1 to 10 and the importance of the items from 1 to 20, with 10 and 20 being the most important. Then they multiply those numbers and have the running order for the day. Keep in mind that you do not want to have too many topics on your agenda.

List agenda items as questions

Would you prefer to join a meeting that has 'budget review' on the agenda or a meeting that has: 'How will we increase our profitability by 10 per cent?' The second meeting sounds a lot more interesting because our brains are wired to want to solve problems and answer questions. Phrase your agenda items as questions, and your participants will be more engaged.

Decide who attends

Now that you know the topics that will be addressed in the meeting, you can decide who needs to be there.

There are two potential problems with the attendee list of your meeting that you need to avoid. One is having too many people in the room. The other one is not having the right people. Let's see how to prevent each of these mistakes.

Avoid having too many attendees

'The more, the merrier' does not apply to meetings. Research has shown that meeting size is negatively related to attendee involvement.[7] It is more stressful to speak up in front of a big group, so you don't. There is no time for everyone to contribute in-depth, so your comments are short and shallow. You become more guarded and less forthcoming. You try to deal with the tough topics before and after the meeting. The meeting itself can become a waste of time.

Bain Consultancy found that you lose 10 per cent of decision-making efficiency for every attendee you have in your meeting above seven.[8] Google tries to limit the number of meeting attendees to ten. Amazon has a 'two pizzas rule': they aim to have meetings with, as a maximum, the number of attendees that two pizzas can feed. At Apple, Steve Jobs was known to interrupt a meeting to kick someone out if he thought that what was being discussed was not relevant to them. He even declined to attend a meeting run by then President Obama because the attendee list was too long.

The science is clear about this, and the tech icons agree. Why, then, do most of us sit through painful meetings with too many attendees? The reasons are mainly psychological and political. People feel excluded and offended when they are not invited to meetings. It is understandable. Our brain, which was developed for thousands of years in the African savannah, thinks that if you are expelled from the tribe, you will die.

In modern-day organizations, meetings are the closest thing we have to a tribe. If you are not invited, all sorts of fight-or-flight responses get activated. Meeting organizers invite too many attendees in order to build a stronger relationship with them and avoid hurting their feelings. So, how can you remove attendees from your meetings without them feeling excluded?

Explain to your team that you are going to make changes in your meetings' size, and that science suggests that smaller meetings are more effective. Address people's social needs so that they do not feel excluded. Explain to people why they are not invited: tell them that you respect their time and prefer them to focus on the other essential projects they work on.

Avoid inviting people who will share similar insights: for example, people from the same department. Ask one person to consult with the rest of the colleagues they represent before the meeting. Ask for some people's input before the meeting so that they do not have to attend, or launch a short survey to gather input from non-attendees. Share the action items and decisions afterwards with the relevant people who did not attend. Reassure people that their views and perspectives will be taken into account by the meeting attendees, even if they do not attend the meeting themselves.

Consider recording the meeting and sharing the recording afterwards. With its culture of radical transparency, Bridgewater Associates records all its business-related, non-proprietary trade meetings so that people who did not attend can watch them and see how a decision was made.

Get the right people in the room

There is something worse than having too many attendees, and that is not having the right people in the room.

As you are deliberating who to invite into a meeting, there are three important roles you need to keep in mind: who decides, who consults, and who performs the work related to the topic at hand. Countless meetings happen without the decision maker present, for example, resulting in wasting everyone's time. The group may deliberate for hours, finally reaching a decision, only to be overruled by the real decision maker. Groups may come up with bad ideas because they do not have the experts in the room or the people who will implement the idea. After a series of wrong decisions, NASA started inviting astronauts to the meetings that decided whether a space shuttle was ready to take off. Having people in the room who could die if the wrong decision was made brought a different, much-needed perspective.

Bring in different perspectives

Consider how you can 'stir the pot' to uncover insights or ideas that would not surface otherwise. Let's say you have a meeting about increasing employee engagement. How about inviting a junior employee or even a former employee to the meeting? When you have a marketing or sales meeting, could you invite a customer? When Virgin was looking to enter the live music sector, they invited musicians to their meetings. One musician they consulted was Jarvis Cocker, the front-man of the band Pulp. He said to Richard Branson that he'd always thought it would be a great idea to hold two festivals on the same weekend in different parts of the country, with a line-up that swaps between the sites over two days. Virgin adopted the idea and ran the V Festival in Britain for more than twenty years.[9]

Encourage diversity of thought

Ask yourself whether you have a diverse enough group. Both demographically but also in terms of expertise and ways of thinking. If your meeting attendees look like clones, it is not set up for success in terms of creative ideas and smart decisions.

Summary

For a successful meeting, you need to craft your agenda carefully and make sure that you have the right people in the room. No observers, only people who will contribute to the meeting's outcome.

Table 9 summarizes the practices we have explored in this chapter to make sure you set up meetings that are designed for success.

| Table 9: Prepare for the Meeting

Form a successful agenda	Decide who attends
Separate strategic from operational meetings	Avoid having too many attendees
State the purpose of the meeting	Get the right people in the room
Seek input to the agenda	
Choose topics that require everyone's participation	Bring in different perspectives
Put the most important topics first	Encourage diversity of thought
List agenda items as questions	

11 Make the Most of Your Virtual Meetings

For many of us, virtual meetings have become the norm rather than the exception. We increasingly work with international teams and partners. The 2020 pandemic caused a rapid transition towards remote work, for many of us overnight. One of the biggest complaints people have about the shift to remote work is virtual meetings.

Virtual meetings come with their own set of opportunities and challenges. The principles shared in this book work, whether you have an in-person or a virtual meeting. Following the 4D Framework and looking after your People and your Process are even more important in virtual meetings, which are more prone to chaos or disengagement. In this chapter, we will explore the nuances of virtual meetings, and some additional strategies to make them successful.

Why virtual meetings are here to stay

The data shows that remote work and virtual meetings can be just as effective as in-person ones, provided we take care of certain important conditions, such as social connectivity, health and our technical toolkit.[1] Research on virtual coaching has found no difference in effectiveness when compared to in-person sessions. And there are a number of benefits when holding virtual meetings.

The right attendees

Virtual meetings make it possible for us to do our work from anywhere in the world. This means we can invite the right people to our meetings, no matter where they are located.

No travel and room costs

Virtual meetings are cheaper and less time consuming. They do not require the rental or use of big meeting rooms. You do not need to pay for travel or spend time in long commutes to attend your meeting. You do not have to postpone virtual meetings because of travel disruptions.

Lower environmental impact

Virtual meetings are better for the environment. The videoconferencing platform Zoom partnered with Chorus.ai platform to measure the environmental impact of in-person versus virtual meetings.[2] They compared an in-person meeting where you had to fly from San Francisco to New York to meet a customer, including hotel stay, with a virtual meeting that you would take from your local office. Their findings are telling. It takes thirty-two trees a year to offset the CO_2 from the one in-person meeting, and it takes one tree just two months to offset the CO_2 from a virtual meeting. We also waste less paper by avoiding printed agendas and documents, which are often thrown into the bin right after our meetings.

Always in the front row

Large meetings can sometimes feel more intimate in a virtual environment. Even though you are far away physically, you can see the speaker up really close on your screen, including their facial expressions, provided they have a good camera and lighting. It is like having a front-row seat. You often get a view of their environment, which can increase a sense of intimacy. If you doubt you can build a strong attachment towards someone you only see on a screen, think about the adoration many people feel towards celebrities and famous people, even if they only ever see them on video.

More equalizing

Some participants describe the experience of virtual meetings as less hierarchical and more equalizing. Everyone takes up the same amount of space on the screen. You just see their head and shoulders. Many factors that could create bias are made invisible, such as your clothes, your body, your shoes, your perfume, your height, your disability, or your build. A client told me that she noticed a difference in how her colleagues treated her during her first pregnancy, when she was in the office, and during her second pregnancy, when she was working remotely and nobody could see her bump in the virtual meetings.

New ways to participate

Virtual meetings give you access to a new set of tools, such as breakouts, virtual whiteboards, online documents, chatbox, surveys and polling. All these can provide new and effective ways of participation. Virtual meetings allow you to record, which enhances transparency. The bar to participate is lower, and that can only be a good thing for people who are shy or more introverted.

Why virtual meetings can be challenging

There are many benefits to virtual meetings. But to make the most of them, we need to be aware of the many challenges.

I was presenting to a potential client to win a big coaching contract. I had walked him through the coaching programme and I had reached the slide with the prices. As luck would have it, my internet connection stopped for a moment and I had to join the meeting again. I felt horrified with what had just happened, but tried to keep calm. I rejoined, and I apologized. I went on to present the pricing slide, and once again I got kicked out. When I rejoined a second time, the client was obviously frustrated. The meeting was running over, and he was tired of waiting for me to log in again and finish my presentation. My company did not get the contract. Things may have been no different if I had not experienced the tech issues, but I am sure they did not help.

Virtual meetings come with their own sets of challenges. Here are some of them.

Tech often fails
We lose the sound, the image freezes, people get disconnected, and they need to join in again. Tech issues can cause a lot of frustration, distraction and stress. They can also get in the way of connecting and communicating effectively. Research shows that when we cannot hear someone clearly, we trust them less. This can penalize a colleague with a dodgy internet connection.

Sound delay
The delay between receiving and sending messages affects our perception of others. A study found that positive answers to

questions (for example, 'Can you give me a ride?', 'Sure') were rated as less genuinely willing if the responder took more than 600 milliseconds to reply.[3] Due to the sound delays in virtual meetings, colleagues who think they are giving forthright answers may come across as reluctant or less genuine.

Less turn-taking and more interruptions

In a virtual environment, participants take fewer turns, mainly due to the sound delay and also because it is harder to recognize the cues that someone else wants to speak. This can reduce the collective intelligence of the group, leading to groupthink. When people choose to speak in a virtual meeting, they will often talk over each other. The sound delay makes it harder to time their turns and also to resolve interruptions quickly.

Less feedback

In a virtual meeting we lack a lot of non-verbal feedback, such as people moving their legs nervously, shuffling their papers, or sighing. The lack of feedback is even worse when we are presenting slides in a virtual environment and cannot even see the participants' faces. We have no idea whether they are nodding, have confused expressions, or are frowning in disagreement. Our jokes are often met with the silence caused by the mute button. It can be unnerving.

Even when you make an effort to look at all your participants' faces, it is hard to interpret their body language from a limited frame on your screen. When you see them looking down and writing something, are they texting on their phone or taking notes? When they look off-screen, are they distracted or trying to listen without visual distraction? When they come closer to the camera, are they attentive or reading an email? Stanford professor Lindred Greer found that conflict in virtual teams escalates more quickly and can be more negative for performance than conflict in teams who are co-located.[4] In virtual communications we often lack the context, and that leads to misunderstandings.

More distractions and disengagement

Our different browser tabs and notifications are calling for our attention while we are in a virtual meeting. If there is a big group, and we can be on mute or with camera off, it is a lot easier to multitask. Remember a time when you talked to someone who was not listening to you and was distracted? It is almost impossible to maintain your train of thought. This happens all too often in virtual meetings.

More tiring

In a face-to-face meeting you pay attention to the speaker, your colleagues, the room and potentially a screen with some slides. In a virtual meeting you have all that, but you also have the different backgrounds of all the speakers, your own image, as well as the chat going on in parallel. There can be an overload of information, and it is exhausting. We are likely to focus on our image on the screen as we want to self-monitor. We may start judging our looks or our expressions in this digital mirror.

What is also tiring is that in virtual meetings we feel we need to constantly look at the screen and the speaker, while in an in-person meeting we would let our eyes wander. There is also less movement from one meeting to the other. Virtual-meeting fatigue is real!

Lack of informal interaction

A big part of the bonding of the participants in an in-person meeting happens when they are walking towards the room, sitting, waiting for the meeting to start, taking breaks, and walking away from the meeting. During a longer meeting, you may also have joint meals with your fellow participants. All this informal interaction is mostly lost in a virtual meeting, unless we make a conscious effort to recreate it.

Eye contact is complicated

Eye contact is important for inspiring trust. For this reason, law scholars and criminal-justice activists have questioned the fairness of remote depositions, hearings and trials.[5] To be perceived as making eye contact, you need to look at the camera. But if you look at the camera, you are not looking at the other participants' faces and you might miss important feedback through their expressions. Ideally, you want to be doing both, alternating your gaze from camera to screen. This dilemma on where you should focus your gaze, unique to virtual meetings, increases the effort we need to exert to simply show up as being fully present.

Too many attendees

Another disadvantage of virtual meetings is that when we are not limited by room capacities, we are tempted to invite too many people. Also, more people are tempted to accept the invitation to virtual meetings even though they may not have the right conditions to fully participate. They assume they can join with the camera and microphone off, and multitask during the meeting. The extended attendee list makes virtual meetings even more challenging.

Lack of touch, taste and smell

It is easy to underestimate how touch can improve our business relationships and inspire trust, whether it is a handshake or a pat on the back. Research has found that waitresses who touch restaurant customers earn more in tips. In an in-person meeting, you can give the participants a product to hold or smell. INSEAD professor Gianpiero Petriglieri has drawn parallels between transitioning to virtual meetings and seances. They are both 'troubled attempts to re-establish a connection with somebody we have lost and still care about, often disturbed by many lost bodies that we care little for and who forget to press mute'. This can be painful. Petriglieri says he finishes his meetings by speaking the truth: 'It was a pleasure being in your absence.'[6]

How to make the most of your virtual meetings

The more bad experiences we have, the lower our expectations are for virtual meetings. The lower our expectations, the less we prepare or set ourselves up in the right conditions to participate in our virtual meetings. The less we prepare for them, the more experiences of bad virtual meetings we have, and this creates a vicious cycle, explains expert virtual-meeting facilitator Judy Rees. If we do not take measures to compensate for the many challenges of virtual meetings, we will end up with even more unsatisfying experiences.

So, how do you take advantage of the opportunities available in virtual meetings and mitigate the challenges? Here are six key strategies.

Shorter, focused meetings and frequent breaks
Virtual meetings can be a lot more tiring than in-person meetings due to sound delay, our need to look at the screen, and information overload. Virtual meetings should be shorter

than equivalent in-person meetings and have frequent breaks. There are people out there running eight-hour virtual meetings with no breaks, and wondering why nobody is paying attention. Judy Rees suggests a five-minute break every hour, and a twenty-minute break every two hours. Also, ask people to stand up, stretch and move about.

Facilitate relationship building

We need to compensate for the loss of informal interaction and sensory closeness, and to build rapport and cohesion in a virtual meeting. Research shows that even five minutes of non-business-related conversation can set the team on a much more positive, productive course.[7] Frequent small breakouts can recreate the informal banter that happens in face-to-face meetings. You can also introduce some fun rituals. A team told me they held a competition of best awkward freezes. When a colleague's image froze in an awkward position, they felt a bit less frustrated as they played the game by taking a screenshot.

If you facilitate a group that is not experienced with virtual meetings, you may want to point out some of the tech limitations. For example, that there are delays sometimes, and they should not be paranoid wondering why they do not get immediate acknowledgement.

Be clear on ground rules

You need to establish ground rules that will set up your virtual meeting for success. Offmute should be your default option, unless you have a big meeting (more than ten people). Mute can be a mood killer, as it hinders spontaneous communication and joint laughter when someone says something funny in the meeting. Ask people in advance to be in a distraction-free space, if possible.

Video is worth having on when there are more than two participants, fewer than thirty, and you want high engagement with each other. Let people know in advance of the meeting if you expect them to have the camera on. You may want to consider having the camera off for some of your one-to-ones, or larger meetings where not much interaction is expected. A study found that lack of eye contact with an interlocutor can increase cognitive performance.[8] That means your one-to-one meetings may be more effective if you do not look at each other, whether you are walking side by side or having a phone conversation instead of a video call. Voice-only meetings can give you the freedom to doodle, stand or walk while you have the conversation. They can also be the best option for meetings with people you do not know well, as they are less intrusive. Being in back-to-back video calls is exhausting, so don't be afraid to ask to switch the camera off when possible and appropriate.

Another ground rule you need to attend to is when and how to use the chat option. I have seen meetings where what's going on in the chat competes with the main meeting, and it can be distracting. Other times, people will say something in the chat in order not to disturb the meeting, but you would much rather they speak up. As a meeting leader, be specific on when and for what reasons you want people to use the chat.

Provide more structure and ways for people to participate

Given the tendency for less turn-taking and more interruptions in virtual meetings, you may want to offer more structure. You can use the round robin, giving each participant the opportunity to contribute without interruptions. You might need to call people by name and ask them to contribute.

As there is a tendency for multitasking during virtual

meetings, it is even more critical to encourage participation. An invitation to participate every five minutes is the minimum to keep your attendees engaged. Ask a question, invite them to write in the chat, answer a poll, write in an online document or on a virtual whiteboard, reflect or go to a breakout room. When you have a bigger group, having breakouts is an excellent strategy to make sure people are engaged and do the work.

Take care of your virtual presence

While a virtual meeting can be forgiving if you choose to wear sweatpants instead of trousers, people will judge what they see on their screen. I was virtually coaching a COO who worked in a skyscraper in the US, and because of the floor-to-ceiling windows behind him I could see only a dark shadow where his face should be. I found it unnerving, and I am sure participants in his virtual meetings felt the same. When I brought this up with him, he admitted he felt more comfortable with the extra 'anonymity' the bad lighting provided. The 'darkness', though, undermined his leadership presence. A £15 LED light could easily solve that problem.

I recommend investing in a good microphone and a good camera. Every YouTuber will tell you to prioritize the microphone over the camera, as people are more forgiving of bad video than bad sound. Use a laptop stand, or even a stack of books, for your computer, so that the camera is at eye level.

Share the facilitation responsibilities

It is a good idea to enlist the help of another participant when you are leading a virtual meeting. You may have technical issues and need someone to take over or tell the participants what to do. You may need someone to admit people from the 'waiting room' while you talk. Have someone else read the chatbox and share with you the most important questions when it is time for Q&A. Or send the participants the link for the document you will work on. Given the increased complexities of a virtual meeting, it is always a good idea to share the facilitation responsibilities.

Summary

Virtual meetings come with benefits but also many challenges. You should be strategic about making the most of them. Follow the strategies shared in this book, by taking care of your Purpose, People and Process.

Table 10 summarizes what we have learned about virtual meetings in this chapter. By bearing in mind the challenges of virtual meetings and mitigating them, you can set yourself up for success.

| Table 10: How to Succeed at Virtual Meetings

Benefits	Disadvantages	Solutions
The right attendees	Tech often fails	Shorter, focused meetings and frequent breaks
No travel and room costs	Sound delay	
	Less turn-taking and more interruptions	Facilitate relationship building
Lower environmental impact	Less feedback	Be clear on ground rules
Always in the front row	More distractions and disengagement	Provide more structure and ways to participate
More equalizing	More tiring	
New ways to participate	Lack of informal interaction	Take care of your virtual presence
	Eye contact is complicated	Share the facilitation responsibilities
	Too many attendees	
	Lack of touch, taste and smell	

12 Start and Finish Your Meeting with Impact

The beginning and the end of your meeting are crucial for its success. A good start will put the attendees in the right frame of mind to achieve the desired outcome. It will centre them with the purpose of the meeting and get them comfortable with each other. Most of us know within the first two minutes of a meeting whether it will be a waste of time. If you are the meeting leader, you need to make a great first impression.

A good ending is as important as a good beginning. It will ensure that participants are clear on what was achieved in the meeting and the next steps. Unless you wrap things up properly, people will move on to the next item in their diary, forgetting what happened in the meeting. As a rule of thumb, I dedicate around 20 to 30 per cent of the meeting's time to the beginning and the end.

How to begin your meeting

The first step in making a great first impression is to start your meeting on time. Steven Rogelberg and his team found that 37 per cent of meetings start late: 'mostly because someone attending was late. This leads to the latecomer feeling rude, while the waiting staffers feel disrespected, upset, and frustrated – all of which drive down performance.'[1]

When you start your meeting, you need to answer the following questions for your attendees.

- Why am I here and why should I care?
- Do I belong here? Am I a valued member of this group?
- How are we going to do this?
- What do I need to know before we get started?

You do that with four steps: centre, connect, contract and consume. Depending on the nature of your meeting, you may want to do all these steps or skip some of them. Let's look at each one in more detail.

| Figure 4: Start Your Meeting with Impact

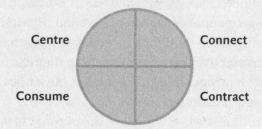

Centre ourselves and focus on the meeting purpose

As the meeting starts, you need to help the participants transition from their frantic day to your meeting – a place to think strategically and creatively.

Non-verbal signals can support this transition. I love to have high-intensity music playing as the participants come into the room or dial in. This small detail has a huge impact. One client commented that he was impressed by how the participants' body language was different as they were waiting for my session to start compared to their usual meetings. They were smiling. The music playing signalled that they would participate in an engaging, fun meeting. You may want to use an inspirational or funny video as people come in, to start getting them in a good mood. Some facilitators use meditation or breathing to help their participants relax and centre themselves before the meeting.

After you have helped the participants become more centred themselves, you need to focus them on the purpose of the meeting. Answer the question 'Why am I here and why should I care?' right at the start. Say something like: 'The purpose of our meeting is . . . and when we are done, we will walk away with . . .' Be clear about which of the four Ds you will cover in the meeting. Are you there to Define a goal or a problem, Develop solutions, Decide the way forward or Do something?

Next, you need to communicate the importance of the discussion, to get people engaged and excited. Patrick Lencioni argues that meetings should be more interesting than movies, as they are interactive and what happens in them has an impact on our lives.[2] It makes sense in theory, but most of us are bored to death in our meetings.

Add some drama when you share the purpose of your meeting and why it is crucial. For example: 'We are here today to discuss which features we are going to create for our product. Our competitors will want us to make the wrong decision. Our clients and shareholders are hoping we make the right one.'

Another way to immediately engage your attendees is to explain what's in it for them. For example: 'After we get clarity on our hiring process, you will save time and recruit better employees for your team.'

Connect with each other

After sharing the purpose of the meeting and why it is important, you need to answer the next two questions: 'Do I belong here?' and 'Am I a valued member of this group?'

Phil Houghton, team coach and partner at Alexander Partnership, told me: 'Teams often want to achieve a big goal. To achieve a big goal, they need to have a big conversation. You cannot have a big conversation in a small relationship.' It is true. Think of what you can achieve when you have a great relationship with someone. The possibilities are limitless. Now think of a colleague with whom you have no relationship, or even a bad relationship. What can you achieve together? The options are significantly fewer.

The beginning of the meeting is a great time to work on improving the relationships among your participants. Don't be tempted to skip this. You may feel you have so much to cover in a limited time that you want to crack on with the agenda. But by spending some time bringing the group together at the beginning of the meeting, you will save a lot of time and money later. Robert Cialdini, world expert on persuasion, tells us that when people like each other, they work better together. He goes on to explain:

> In a series of negotiation studies carried out between MBA students at two well-known business schools, some groups were told, 'Time is money. Get straight down to business.' In this group, around 55 per cent were able to come to an agreement. A second group, however, was told, 'Before you begin negotiating, exchange some personal information with each other. Identify a similarity you share in common, then begin negotiating.' In this group, 90 per cent of them

were able to come to successful and agreeable outcomes that were typically worth 18 per cent more to both parties.[3]

Personal, positive, vulnerable

Connecting does not need to take a lot of time. At the beginning of the meeting, have a participatory activity that will allow people to communicate with each other at a human level. Ideally, you want to get everyone's voice heard in the first three minutes of the meeting.

You can have participants share something personal, positive or vulnerable.

- By sharing something **personal**, the participants will humanize each other.
- Sharing something **positive** will help the group get into a positive mood, and therefore think more expansively and more creatively.[4]
- Sharing something **vulnerable** at the beginning of the meeting can boost the meeting's success.

Management professor Leigh Thompson found that groups who shared funny or embarrassing stories about themselves at the beginning of their meeting came up with 26 per cent more ideas than those groups who didn't.[5] By starting the meeting sharing some vulnerable information about themselves, the participants are more likely to ask questions, admit mistakes and suggest ideas without the fear of looking stupid later.

While positivity is good at the beginning of the meeting, we need to be careful not to force it on participants, and that's where sharing something vulnerable can be beneficial. It makes it OK for the participants to be themselves and not feel that they need to mask their emotions with a veneer of positivity.

'Meeting attendees who feel the need to mask their emotional reactions get less from the meeting itself, and are more likely to experience negative long-term outcomes such as burnout,' found Dr Linda Shanock and her team.[6]

You can find a list of fun, personal or vulnerable questions and exercises to do at the beginning of your meetings in the Appendix.

Take the emotional temperature

Sometimes the initial exercise can reveal something more important to work on than the existing agenda. I was coaching a leadership team during the lockdown due to the Covid-19 crisis. Times were tough, both financially and emotionally, for the leaders. For the initial Connect exercise I asked them to share the highlight and the lowlight of their last month. Many of the participants in the meeting mentioned the same event as a lowlight: the day the company had to make redundancies. Many of them described it as a traumatic event. The leader of the team reacted defensively. She could not understand. Only one of the executives in the meeting had had to make members of his team redundant. The leader felt betrayed, as she had worked so hard to minimize the redundancies, but she felt that the team of executives was criticizing her instead of supporting her.

We had a packed agenda for the day and when I saw all this raw emotion coming into the meeting, I felt a glimpse of worry. Would this tension derail the meeting? Should I move on with the agenda? I named what I saw: 'The team obviously has some intense emotions around this topic.' This comment itself helped the participants step away for a moment from the intense emotion and observe it. I asked for a five-minute break. When people came back, I had them anonymously do a retrospective on a virtual whiteboard. They were to add virtual Post-its in two areas, answering two questions. What had gone well in the way they had handled the recent crisis? What would they need to do differently in the future?

The leader of the team looked relieved to see all the things the team believed had gone well. She did not feel so criticized any more. The team also felt relieved, because they were able to speak up about the things that should have happened in a different way. After this exercise they felt in the right emotional state to tackle the agenda, and the team was ready to move on with the rest of the meeting.

Contract on the how

Your participants will want to have an idea of how you are going to work together to achieve the meeting's purpose. Contracting has two parts: the group agreement, and the facilitator agreement.

Group agreement

A group agreement is common in coaching and training, but it is terribly absent in the day-to-day workplace. Have the group discuss and come up with an agreement on how you want to behave with each other in this meeting, whether it is a recurring or a one-off event. You decide what atmosphere you wish to create between you. Here are some examples of ground rules you can have in your group agreement.

- Be honest
- Respect each other
- Have fun
- Share all the information I think is relevant
- Focus on needs, not positions

You will also need to discuss your meeting etiquette. Are interruptions allowed or discouraged? What about technology? Can people be on their phone or their laptops during the meeting? If you are the team leader, make sure you model the behaviour you want to see in others. If the boss does electronic multitasking in a meeting, other attendees are 2.2 times more likely to do so as well.[7]

You do not need to formulate a group agreement in every meeting. You can do it once and then refer to it in subsequent meetings. When you start a new meeting, you may want to remind people of a particular point from the agreement that is especially relevant to the issue at hand. For example: 'The stakes are high for our topic today, so we need to pay attention to the part of our agreement about participation. I want to hear everyone.' By creating a group agreement, you help the group take ownership for the success of the meeting rather than shouldering all the burden yourself.

A technique I learned from coach Irini Nikolaidou is to ask a volunteer from the group to write down observations about whether the team agreement is respected and share them with the group at the end of the meeting. This creates a feedback mechanism until the agreement is ingrained in the behaviour of the team. Nikolaidou observes that after the first couple of meetings, the team learns to stick to the ground rules.

The contract stage is where you also get agreement on the agenda. By doing so, you get your attendees' commitment to the plan, and it is less likely they will stray off-topic. Explain how you will tackle the agenda items: use of breakouts, Post-it notes, etc.

Facilitator agreement

After you have completed the group agreement, ask the group about their expectations of you, as the meeting leader, and write them down on a facilitator agreement. Groups may ask you to help keep them focused on the agenda. They may want your support to ensure all voices are heard. Hearing these expectations will make your job as a facilitator easier. You will have permission from the group to intervene as you see fit to make the meeting a success.

Consume the relevant information

Amazon teams start their strategic meetings by giving fifteen minutes for people to read a memo that someone has prepared about the issue at hand. This replaces the PowerPoint that most companies use for internal quarterly reviews, proposals, etc.

Jack Dorsey, Twitter CEO, starts most of his meetings with everyone reading and commenting on a Google doc for ten minutes. 'This practice makes time for everyone to get on the same page, allows us to work from many locations, and gets to truth/critical thinking faster,' he tweeted.[8]

The benefits of reading versus presenting are multiple. People consume the information at their own pace rather than having someone dictating the same pace for everyone. Participants who prepare the memo need to go deeper, as they cannot hide behind beautiful slides and bullet points. Everyone is on the same page and you ensure that they have the time to read the information, which does not always happen when you send it in advance. If you have a lot of information that you would like the group to consume to achieve the purpose of the meeting, consider the written memo.

Do not send the information in advance and then still go through it during the meeting. People who have prepared will be bored and feel the meeting is wasting their time. Next time, nobody will prepare. Either send the information in advance or allow time for reading at the beginning of the meeting, but not both.

How to end your meeting with intention

The time is running out, and you are still in the middle of the conversation. You are trying to close the discussion, feeling bad for interrupting. You are striving to create some agreement on the next steps, but there is simply not enough time as people start packing up to go to their next meeting or post in the chat that they need to go. And then they are gone. You are left behind with the feeling that your meeting was a failure.

Does the above scenario resonate? Most meeting leaders tend to run out of time, and they do not wrap up the meeting properly. Ending the meeting well is important. Leave time for the closure exercises. For example, say: 'We have gone as far as we can today. Now we need to start wrapping up the meeting.'

Finishing on time is important. I have to admit, I used to struggle with it. I loved my team coaching sessions, and I wanted the group to get as much value out of them as possible. I thought I was delivering that little bit extra as a coach by staying between five and ten minutes longer. I could not have been more wrong.

On one occasion, my delay in finalizing the meeting resulted in a near disaster. We were supposed to finish the team coaching session at 6 p.m., and we had a dinner reservation at 7 p.m. As there was an hour gap, I thought I could let the meeting run over a bit, as we were doing important work. We were at an offsite venue in a co-working space.

The venue manager started complaining at exactly 6 p.m. By

the time we finished, at 6.10, she had left and locked the building. We started wandering around the dark corridors, trying to locate an exit. I felt embarrassed. We finally managed to find a way out, but I learned my lesson. People feel frustrated when meetings overrun. I now always finish my meetings on time. And I suggest you do too.

We need to achieve three things when we end a meeting:

- alignment on where the group is
- clarity on what happens next, and
- recognition of the value created.

Let's review how you can achieve these in your meetings.

Alignment on where the group is

Participants often leave a meeting without being clear on what was agreed. Even worse, they may leave a meeting determined not to do what was agreed, or even to sabotage it. I suggest you write down the decisions that have been made in the meeting. Then ask: 'Is everyone OK with where we have ended up?' Writing the decisions down and getting a verbal agreement will help you avoid misunderstandings.

Check for completion by asking something like this: 'Is there anything else someone needs to say or ask before we end the meeting?' If you do not, people may have hallway or direct-messaging conversations about it.

If people disagree, but the decision is final, it is useful to get their commitment that they will support the decision once they have left the meeting. Otherwise, they may share their disagreement widely and sabotage the decision.

Clarity on what happens next

Everyone needs to leave a meeting with clarity about the next steps. Agree on who will do what, by when. You may also want to set a date for the next meeting and develop a preliminary agenda. Discuss who needs to be informed about the decisions taken in the meeting, and how you will go about doing that. This is especially crucial for important, strategic meetings.

Recognition of the value created

A lot of value is created in meetings, if they are run correctly. But without taking a moment to reflect on it and capture it, it gets lost. You may want to ask the participants what their key takeaway was, and what they thought of the meeting. Research shows that companies who have a habit of asking attendees to rate a meeting, raise the quality of their meetings.[9] Professor Peter Hawkins suggests that, for longer meetings, you check how things are going at the midpoint. You can ask something like: 'What is the most important value we have created together so far, and what do we need to do differently in the second half of the meeting?'

I like finishing all my meetings with a short closing round. I got the idea from Ev Williams, co-founder of Twitter and Medium. You go round and ask everyone to comment on the meeting in thirty seconds or less. There is no back-and-forth. Ev Williams argues that:

The closing round is worth doing, because it gives everyone, in a sense, a 'last word' – the chance to get something off their chest that they might otherwise carry around or whisper to their colleagues later. It creates more mindfulness about what just happened – and how things might go better next time.[10]

Participants also get an opportunity to share how they feel about the direction of the group. Another lovely way to end the meeting is to ask participants to share one thing they have appreciated in the person sitting to their right at the table or on the screen. This will ensure that your relationships are strengthened, and people leave your meeting with a warm fuzzy feeling and a better sense of belonging.

Summary

In this chapter, we have looked at how best to start and finish your meetings. Table 11 summarizes the strategies you need to remember.

| Table 11: Starting and Finishing the Meeting

Start the meeting	Finish the meeting
Centre: Why am I here and why should I care?	Alignment on where the group is
Connect: Do I belong here? Am I a valued member of this group?	Clarity on what happens next
	Recognition of the value created
Contract: How are we going to do this?	
Consume: What do I need to know?	

Moving Forward

If someone had told me a few years ago, when I felt overwhelmed at the thought of joining another meeting, that now I would love coaching teams and I would be an advocate for successful meetings, I would have struggled to believe it. The pain I was feeling was not just boredom, or frustration for the time wasted. It was a pain born of feeling disconnected, even though I was speaking to people the whole day.

I launched my company to help leaders who felt overwhelmed and disconnected to maximize their impact and sense of fulfilment. Soon enough, I realized that when you are seeking impact and fulfilment, fixing your meetings is a great place to start. Meetings allow you to bring people together in real time to make a difference. When you have successful meetings, you feel connected, valued and powerful – and so do your participants.

The quality of our meetings will determine the impact of our career. If we look at the global trends, holding successful meetings is becoming an ever more important skill. As robots take over most mechanical and analytical jobs, it is our ability to bring people together to uncover insights and creatively solve the most pressing problems that will set us apart. As more people work remotely, successful meetings that connect people across the globe become ever more important. As society polarizes further – in part, due to the one-sided, personalized information we get in our social media feeds – bringing people together in participatory, diverse meetings to work collaboratively may be our best bet towards a better future.

To hold successful meetings, we need to take care of their Purpose, People and Process. A successful meeting is a meeting that Defines, Develops, Decides or Does successfully. Let's welcome the People in our meetings in a way that enables everyone to bring their true selves and speak their minds, even when it is uncomfortable. Finally, the Process with which we create and design our meetings matters.

Now you have reached the end of the book, take some time to journal or reflect on what you have learned, before you move on and start looking forward in your career.

If you have enjoyed this book, please consider writing a review to help other people find it. I would love to read what you thought of it. I would also love to hear from you directly. You can write to me about anything related to leadership, personal development and, of course, meetings, at LinkedIn, Facebook or Twitter @ckostoula.

I have also created a bonus for you on the www.theleaderpath. com/meetings website: a pdf with the technical tools I use in my meetings (ideation platforms, virtual whiteboards, collaboration tools, word-cloud creators, etc.).

If you want to get personalized feedback on your meetings, go to www.theleaderpath.com/meetings and take the quiz 'How Successful Are Your Meetings?' Feel free to send it to your colleagues.

It is time to ask more from our workday than it being an endless grind of soulless meetings. Holding successful meetings is an act of love. You make a difference by creating connection, uncovering insights, unleashing creativity and getting things done. Every major change in human history started with a meeting.

Let's go out, bring people together in successful meetings, and change the world for the better!

Acknowledgements

This book would not exist without my editor at Penguin Random House, Celia Buzuk. She reached out a few months after I had decided I wanted to write a book to ask me to contribute to the Penguin Business Expert series. I felt like she was my fairy godmother, magically appearing at the right moment. It was a joy working with her, from choosing the topic to completing the manuscript.

I interviewed a series of world-class experts for this book, including David Clutterbuck, Georgina Woudstra, Giorgos Vareloglou, Irini Nikolaidou, Judy Rees, Marc Zornes, Peter Hawkins and Phil Houghton. Their insights enriched it immeasurably. Many others' research and thoughts contributed too; you will find a long list of references. This book indeed stands on the shoulders of giants.

A huge thank you to all the amazing humans who read the first version of the manuscript and provided the invaluable feedback that shaped it: Ann Maynard, Anne de Kerckhove, Matthias Kunze, Petros Oratis and Simon Birkenhead.

Another fantastic group, including Angelos Derlopas, Lauren Taylor, Michalis Rikakis, Nikos Dimos and Sokratis Vidros, did the second-round beta-reading: thank you!

For the feedback on specific chapters, I am grateful to Christos Manolis, Constantine Karampatsos, Judy Rees, Nayem Chowdhury and Zaharenia Atzitzikaki.

It was during one of Lucy McCarraher's book-writing workshops that I put the book's chapter structure together. Lucy: using cards for this process works!

A huge thanks to copy-editor Shân Morley Jones and editorial manager Ellie Smith for getting the manuscript ready to publish.

This book would not exist without my clients, who trusted the Leaderpath team and me to help them pursue impact and fulfilment, while fixing some of their meetings in the process.

I wanted to thank my coaching supervisor Erik de Haan who has been supporting me to become a better coach for years. Also, my business mentors Angus Ridgway and Ann de Kerckhove, who have volunteered their time to provide me with invaluable guidance.

A huge thank you to my accountability group: Chris Blackwell, Jonny Murton, Mark Purdy, Michael Brigo, Sarah Holland and Sharon Summer. I still remember the desperate message I sent you when I realized that I needed to write the book during lockdown while homeschooling my children. Your support was vital.

My mum Olga Rakka, dad Ioannis Kostoulas and two brothers Nikos and Giorgos Kostoulas have been there to cheer me up through the emotional rollercoaster of writing a book. Your vision about what this book could achieve provided endless inspiration.

My two children Sofia and Christos Kofodimos fill my heart with joy and pride every single day, and I cannot wait for them to be old enough to read this book. Kids, I love you.

Finally, I want to thank my husband Dimitrios Kofodimos, for covering at home, listening, proofreading and supporting, to help make this book a success. I could not have asked for a better life partner.

Appendix

Questions and exercises to do at the beginning of your meetings to connect.

1 Where were you born?
2 How many siblings do you have, and where are you in the birth order?
3 Share a particular challenge you had growing up.
4 What was the best and the worst part of last week/month/etc.?
5 Share an embarrassing story from your career.
6 If you could be guaranteed one thing in life (besides money and health), what would it be?
7 If you could change places with anyone in the world, who would it be and why?
8 What would the title of your autobiography be?
9 What is the best advice you were ever given?
10 What would you do if you won the lottery?
11 What did you do at the weekend?
12 Share photos of your latest trip.
13 Describe with one word how you feel.
14 Rank from 1 to 10 how positive or energized you feel.
15 What was your first job? (For large virtual meetings ask participants to change their screen name to that.)

16 Bring to the meeting an object that is meaningful to you, to show to your participants.

17 Draw a self-portrait with your past, present and future, and show it to the team.

18 Draw a self-portrait with what is in your mind and your heart, and show it to the participants.

Endnotes

(All websites listed in the notes were accessed in January 2021.)

Introduction

1. https://www.clarizen.com/press-release/clarizen-survey-workers-consider-status-meetings-a-productivity-killing-waste-of-time/.
2. *Doodle State of Meetings Report 2019*: 'Financial impact of meetings: The cost of poorly organised meetings': https://meeting-report.com/.
3. Abigail Hess, '67% of workers say spending too much time in meetings distracts them from doing their job', CNBC 17 November 2019.

1 Meetings Matter

1. See the Tremendous Leadership website: https://tremendousleadership.com/pages/charlie.
2. Mankins et al, 'Your Scarcest Resource', *Harvard Business Review*, May 2014.
3. Michael Mankins, 'This Weekly Meeting Took Up 300,000 Hours a Year', *Harvard Business Review*, April 2014.
4. Paul Graham, 'Maker's Schedule, Manager's Schedule': http://www.paulgraham.com/makersschedule.html.
5. Peter Rubinstein, 'Blame your worthless workdays on "meeting recovery syndrome"', BBC *WorkLife*, 12 November 2019.
6. Rogelberg et al, 2010, 'Employee Satisfaction with Meetings: A Contemporary Facet of Job Satisfaction', *Human Resource Management*, 49 (2), 149–72.

7. Alexandra Luong and Steven G. Rogelberg, 2005, 'Meetings and More Meetings: The Relationship Between Meeting Load and the Daily Well-Being of Employees', *Group Dynamics Theory Research and Practice*, 9 (1), 58–67.
8. Leach et al, 2009, 'Perceived Meeting Effectiveness: The Role of Design Characteristics', *Journal of Business and Psychology*, 24 (1), 65–76.
9. Steven G. Rogelberg, 'Why Your Meetings Stink – and What to Do About It', *Harvard Business Review*, January 2019.

2 The 4D Meeting Framework

1. Al Pittampalli, 'Why Groups Struggle to Solve Problems Together', *Harvard Business Review*, November 2019.
2. *Doodle State of Meetings Report 2019*: 'Meetings organisation: Key elements of successful meetings': https://meeting-report.com/.

3 Define the Problem or the Goal

1. Sohrab et al, 2015, 'Exploring the Hidden-Profile Paradigm: A Literature Review and Analysis', *Small Group Research*, 46 (5), 1–47.
2. https://www.theventuremag.com/conflict-collaboration/.
3. Peter Hawkins is the author of *Leadership Team Coaching: Developing Collective Transformational Leadership*, Kogan Page, 2017.
4. Thomas Wedell-Wedellsborg, 'Are You Solving the Right Problems?', *Harvard Business Review*, January 2017.
5. Stefan Thomke and Donald Reinertsen, 'Six Myths of Product Development', *Harvard Business Review*, May 2012.
6. Caterina Kostoula, 'How To Design Performance Reviews That Don't Fail Women', *Fast Company*, 22 January 2018.
7. Thomas Wedell-Wedellsborg, 'Are You Solving the Right Problems?', *Harvard Business Review*, January 2017.

4 Develop Ideas

1. Germünden, H. G., and Hauschildt, J., 1985, 'Number of alternatives and efficiency in different types of top-management decisions', *European Journal of Operational Research*, 22 (2), 178–90.

2. See Winnow's website: https://www.winnowsolutions.com/ company.

3. Wuchty et al, 2007, 'The Increasing Dominance of Teams in Production of Knowledge', *Science*, 316 (58), 1036-9.

4. George Land, 'The Failure of Success', TEDx Tucson Talk, December 2011, at: https://www.youtube.com/watch? v=ZFKMq-rYtnc.

5. Kruglanski et al, 2006, 'Groups as epistemic providers: Need for closure and the unfolding of group-centrism', *Psychological Review*, 113 (1), 84-100.

6. Teresa Amabile and Mukti Khaire, 'Creativity and the Role of the Leader', *Harvard Business Review*, October 2008.

7. Mullen et al, 2010, 'Productivity Loss in Brainstorming Groups: A Meta-Analytic Integration', *Basic and Applied Social Psychology*, 12 (1), 3-23.

8. Dennis, A. R., and Williams, M. L., 2005, 'A Meta-Analysis of Group Side Effects in Electronic Brainstorming: More Heads are Better than One', *IJeC*, 1 (1), 24-42.

9. Camacho, L. M., and Paulus, P. B., 1995, 'The role of social anxiousness in group brainstorming', *Journal of Personality and Social Psychology*, 68 (6), 1071-80.

10. Girotra et al, *Idea Generation and the Quality of the Best Idea*, INSEAD Faculty & Research Working Paper, 2008.

11. DeRosa et al, 2007, 'The medium matters: Mining the long-promised merit of group interaction in creative idea generation tasks in a meta-analysis of the electronic group brainstorming literature', *Computers in Human Behavior*, 23 (3), 1549-81.

12. For two particularly useful academic studies on the ineffectiveness and inefficiency of traditional brainstorming, see (1) Paul A. Mongeau, 'The Brainstorming Myth', Annual Meeting of the Western States Communication Association, Albuquerque, New Mexico, 15 February 1993; and (2) Fredric M. Jablin and David R. Seibold, 1978, 'Implications for problem-solving groups of empirical research on "brainstorming": A critical review of the literature', *Southern Speech Communication Journal*, 43 (4), 327-56.

186   Endnotes

13. See Kevin Coyne and Shawn Coyne, *Brainsteering: A Better Approach to Breakthrough Ideas*, HarperBusiness, 2011.
14. Linsey et al, 2011, 'An Experimental Study of Group Idea Generation Techniques: Understanding the Roles of Idea Representation and Viewing Methods', *Journal of Mechanical Design*, 133 (3), 031008 (15 pages).
15. Art Markman, 'Your Team Is Brainstorming All Wrong', *Harvard Business Review*, May 2017.
16. See IDEO's website at https://designthinking.ideo.com/.

5 Decide the Way Forward

1. De Smet et al, 'Untangling your organization's decision making', *McKinsey Quarterly*, 21 June 2017.
2. Dan Lovallo and Daniel Kahneman, 'Delusions of Success: How Optimism Undermines Executives' Decisions', *Harvard Business Review*, July 2003.
3. Erik Larson, 'New Research: Diversity + Inclusion = Better Decision Making At Work', *Forbes*, 21 September 2017.
4. Dan Lovallo and Olivier Sibony, 'The case for behavioral strategy', *McKinsey Quarterly*, 1 March 2010.
5. See Erin Meyer's well-researched book, *The Culture Map: Decoding How People Think, Lead, and Get Things Done Across Cultures*, PublicAffairs, 2016.
6. Paul Ziobro, 'Floundering Mattel Tries to Make Things Fun Again', *Wall Street Journal*, 22 December 2014.
7. McLeod, S. A., 'Solomon Asch – Conformity Experiment' (28 December 2018). Retrieved from https://www.simplypsychology.org/asch-conformity.html.
8. https://www.aboutamazon.com/news/company-news/2016-letter-to-shareholders.
9. W. Chan Kim and Renée Mauborgne, 'Fair Process: Managing in the Knowledge Economy', *Harvard Business Review*, January 2003.
10. Richard M. Rosen and Fred Adair, 'CEOs Misperceive Top Teams' Performance', *Harvard Business Review*, September 2007.

11. McKinsey & Company Podcast, 16 August 2019: https://
www.mckinsey.com/business-functions/strategy-and-
corporate-finance/our-insights/how-to-beat-your-biases-and-
make-better-investment-decisions.

12. Lightle et al, 2009, 'Information Exchange in Group Decision
Making: The Hidden Profile Problem Reconsidered', *Management
Science*, 55 (4), 568–81.

13. Lu et al, 2012, 'Twenty-five years of hidden profiles in group
decision making: A meta-analysis', *Personality and Social Psychology
Review*, 16 (1), 54–75.

14. David H. Zhu, 2013, 'Group polarization on corporate boards:
Theory and evidence on board decisions about acquisition
premiums', *Strategic Management Journal*, 34 (7), 800–822.

15. https://examples.yourdictionary.com/examples-of-groupthink.html.

16. Aaron Hermann and Hussain Gulzar Rammal, 2010, 'The
grounding of the "flying bank"', *Management Decision*, 48 (7),
1048–62.

17. Hal Arkes and Catherine Blumer, 1985, 'The psychology of sunk
cost', *Organizational Behavior and Human Decision Processes*,
35 (1), 124–40.

18. Freek Vermeulen and Niro Sivanathan, 'Stop Doubling Down
on Your Failing Strategy', *Harvard Business Review*, November–
December 2017.

19. See Meyer, *The Culture Map*, Chapter 7, 'The Needle, Not the Knife:
Disagreeing Productively', pp. 195–218.

20. Gary Klein, 'Performing a Project Premortem', *Harvard Business
Review*, September 2007.

21. Mitchell et al, 1989, 'Back to the future: Temporal perspective in
the explanation of events', *Journal of Behavioral Decision Making*,
2 (1), 25–38.

22. Jack Zenger and Joseph Folkman, 'The Ideal Praise-to-Criticism
Ratio', *Harvard Business Review*, March 2013.

23. Marshall B. Rosenberg, *Nonviolent Communication: A Language
of Life – Life-Changing Tools for Healthy Relationships*, 3rd edition,
PuddleDancer Press, 2015.

24. Eisenhardt et al, 'How Management Teams Can Have a Good Fight', *Harvard Business Review*, July–August 1997.

25. Jennifer Aaker and Naomi Bagdonas, *Humour, Seriously: Why Humour is a Superpower at Work and in Life*, Penguin Business, 2020.

26. https://www.gottman.com/blog/the-four-horsemen-recognizing-criticism-contempt-defensiveness-and-stonewalling/.

27. https://www.bain.com/insights/score-your-organization-ame-info/.

6 Do! Execute, Plan and Inspire for Action

1. https://www.hackerearth.com/community-hackathons/resources/e-books/guide-to-organize-hackathon/.

2. https://sprintstories.com/launching-a-direct-to-consumer-business-in-3-days-in-austria-c67d3da7ff5f.

3. https://www.sydneyoperahouse.com/our-story/sydney-opera-house-facts.html.

4. B. Drummond Ayres Jr, 'Finally, 16 Months Late, Denver Has a New Airport', *New York Times*, 1 March 1995.

5. Dan Lovallo and Daniel Kahneman, 'Delusions of Success: How Optimism Undermines Executives' Decisions', *Harvard Business Review*, July 2003.

6. https://www.researchgate.net/publication/281461096_The_Principle_of_the_Malevolent_Hiding_Hand_or_the_Planning_Fallacy_Writ_Large.

7. Buehler et al, 2010, 'The Planning Fallacy: Cognitive, Motivational, and Social Origins', *Advances in Experimental Social Psychology*, 43, 1–62.

8. Peter M. Gollwitzer, 1999, 'Implementation Intentions: Strong Effects of Simple Plans', *American Psychologist*, 54 (7), 493–503.

9. Heidi Grant, 'Get Your Team to Do What It Says It's Going to Do', *Harvard Business Review*, May 2014.

10. Grant, 'Get Your Team to Do What It Says'.

11. Freek Vermeulen and Niro Sivanathan, 'Stop Doubling Down on Your Failing Strategy', *Harvard Business Review*, November–December 2017.

12. Forsyth, D. K., 2008, 'Allocating time to future tasks: The effect of task segmentation on planning fallacy bias', *Memory & Cognition*, 36 (4), 791–8.

13. Lovallo and Kahneman, 'Delusions of Success'.

14. Lisa B. Kwan, 'The Collaboration Blind Spot', *Harvard Business Review*, March–April 2019.

15. Daniel H. Pink, *Drive: The Surprising Truth about What Motivates Us*, Canongate Books, 2010.

16. Lerner et al, 2015, 'Emotion and Decision Making', *Annual Review of Psychology*, 66, 799–823.

7 Connect with Others

1. Nadler et al, 2010, 'Better Mood and Better Performance: Learning Rule-Described Categories Is Enhanced by Positive Mood', *Psychological Science*, 21 (12), 1770–76.

2. https://www.sciencedaily.com/releases/2008/02/080208172104.htm.

3. Jessica Lakin and Tanya Chartrand, 2003, 'Using Nonconscious Behavioral Mimicry to Create Affiliation and Rapport', *Psychological Science*, 14 (4), 334–9.

4. Alicke et al (eds), *The Self in Social Judgement*, Psychology Press, 2005, pp 83–106.

5. https://www.cnbc.com/2017/10/04/warren-buffett-says-this-one-investment-supersedes-all-others.html.

6. https://a16z.com/2012/08/30/one-on-one/.

7. Julie Zhuo, *The Making of a Manager: What to Do When Everyone Looks to You*, Virgin Books, 2019, p. 61.

8. https://www.linkedin.com/company/hollisco.

8 Ensure That People Speak Up in Your Meetings

1. Woolley et al, 2010, 'Evidence of a Collective Intelligence Factor in the Performance of Human Groups', *Science*, 330 (6004), 686–8.

2. https://www.advisory.com/daily-briefing/2017/07/07/men-interrupting-women.

3. Sean R. Martin, 'Research: Men Get Credit for Voicing Ideas, but Not Problems. Women Don't Get Credit for Either', *Harvard Business Review*, November 2017.

4. Joan C. Williams and Sky Mihaylo, 'How the Best Bosses Interrupt Bias on Their Teams, *Harvard Business Review*, November–December 2019.

5. Linda L. Carli, 2001, 'Gender and Social Influence', *Journal of Social Issues*, 57 (4), 725–41.

6. Human Rights Campaign Foundation, *A Workplace Divided: Understanding the Climate for LGBTQ Workers Nationwide*, survey carried out in February and March 2018, p. 6.

7. https://www.cipd.co.uk/news-views/viewpoint/race-inclusion-workplace.

8. McCluney et al, 'The Costs of Code-Switching', *Harvard Business Review*, November 2019.

9. Juliet Bourke and Andrea Titus, 'The Key to Inclusive Leadership', *Harvard Business Review*, March 2020.

10. Juliet Bourke and Andrea Titus, 'Why Inclusive Leaders Are Good for Organizations, and How to Become One', *Harvard Business Review*, March 2019.

11. Heath et al, 'Women, Find Your Voice', *Harvard Business Review*, June 2014.

12. Karen Ruhleder and Brigitte Jordan, 2001, 'Co-Constructing Non-Mutual Realities: Delay-Generated Trouble in Distributed Interaction', *Computer Supported Cooperative Work*, 10 (1), 113–38.

13. Juliet Eilperin of the *Washington Post*, quoted in Emily Crockett, 'The amazing tool that women in the White House used to fight gender bias', *Vox*, 14 September 2016.

14. https://knowledge.insead.edu/strategy/what-could-have-saved-nokia-and-what-can-other-companies-learn-3220.

15. Gretchen Gavett, 'Can GM Make it Safe for Employees to Speak Up?', *Harvard Business Review*, June 2014.

16. Ed Catmull, 'How Pixar Fosters Collective Creativity', *Harvard Business Review*, September 2008.

9 Reduce the Time Wasted in Meetings

1. https://www.payscale.com/career-news/2016/07/science-says-best-day-time-meeting.

2. https://www.inc.com/rebecca-hinds-and-bob-sutton/dropbox-secret-for-saving-time-in-meetings.html.

3. https://www.inc.com/jeff-haden/mark-cuban-says-there-is-only-1-reason-he-will-agree-to-a-business-meeting-its-pure-genius.html.

4. https://www.clarizen.com/press-release/clarizen-survey-workers-consider-status-meetings-a-productivity-killing-waste-of-time/.

5. Kevin Kruse, LEADx CEO, Facebook post, 4 April 2020.

6. Mankins et al, 'Your Scarcest Resource', *Harvard Business Review*, May 2014.

7. Ben Waber, *People Analytics: How Social Sensing Technology Will Transform Business and What It Tells Us about the Future of Work*, FT Analytics/Prentice Hall, 2013.

8. Alex 'Sandy' Pentland, 'The New Science of Building Great Teams', *Harvard Business Review*, April 2012.

9. Mankins et al, 'Your Scarcest Resource'.

10 Prepare for a Successful Meeting

1. https://journal.accj.or.jp/peter-drucker-on-leadership.

2. https://articles.uie.com/perspectives_over_power/.

3. Leach et al, 2009, 'Perceived Meeting Effectiveness: The Role of Design Characteristics', *Journal of Business Psychology*, 24 (1), 65–76.

4. Michael Mankins, 'Stop Wasting Valuable Time', *Harvard Business Review*, September 2004.

5. https://www.thefreelibrary.com/Inside+Intel%27s+meeting+culture.-a055007185.

6. Littlepage, G. E., and Poole, J. R., 1993, 'Time allocation in decision making groups', *Journal of Social Behavior & Personality*, 8 (4), 663–72.

7. Leach et al, 'Perceived Meeting Effectiveness'.

8. https://www.bain.com/insights/decision-insights-9-decision-focused-meetings/.

9. https://mainstottawa.com/richard-branson-three-ways-to-innovate-better-ideas/.

11 Make the Most of Your Virtual Meetings

1. https://www.bcg.com/publications/2020/valuable-productivity-gains-covid-19.
2. https://blog.zoom.us/how-video-meetings-are-helping-reduce-environmental-impact-infographic/.
3. Roberts et al, 2006, 'The interaction of inter-turn silence with prosodic cues in listener perceptions of "trouble" in conversation', *Speech Communication*, 48 (9), 1079–93.
4. Deborah Petersen, 'Lindred Greer: Why Virtual Teams Have More Conflict', *Insights by Stanford Business*, November 2014.
5. Anne Bowen Poulin, 2004, 'Criminal Justice and Videoconferencing Technology: The Remote Defendant', *Tulane Law Review*, 78, 1115–18.
6. Gianpiero Petriglieri, 'We are all Zoombies now, but it has to stop', *Financial Times*, 14 May 2020.
7. Leigh Thompson, '5 Tips for Making a Good Impression – Virtually', *Harvard Business Review*, April 2020.
8. Lucy Markson, 2009, 'Effects of gaze-aversion on visual-spatial imagination', *British Journal of Psychology*, 100 (3), 553–63.

12 Start and Finish Your Meeting with Impact

1. https://bps-research-digest.blogspot.com/2013/03/the-scourge-of-meeting-late-comers.html.
2. Patrick Lencioni, *Death by Meeting: A Leadership Fable About Solving the Most Painful Problem in Business*, Jossey-Bass, 2004.
3. https://www.influenceatwork.com/principles-of-persuasion/#liking.
4. https://www.sciencedaily.com/releases/2010/12/101215113253.htm.
5. Leigh Thompson, 'Research: For Better Brainstorming, Tell an Embarrassing Story', *Harvard Business Review*, October 2017.
6. Shanock et al, 2013, 'Less acting, more doing: How surface acting relates to perceived meeting effectiveness and other employee outcomes', *Journal of Occupational and Organizational Psychology*, 86 (4), 457–76.

7. Fuller et al, 'If You Multitask During Meetings, Your Team Will, Too', *Harvard Business Review*, January 2018.

8. Jack Dorsey, @jack Tweet, 20 April 2018.

9. Steven G. Rogelberg, 'Why Your Meetings Stink – and What to Do About It', *Harvard Business Review*, January 2019.

10. https://medium.com/@ev/how-to-end-every-meeting-a0b7bc1eb86f.

Index